Sense and Non-Sense

Sense and Non-Sense

American Culture and Politics

J. Harry Wray

DePaul University

Upper Saddle River
New Jersey 07458

Library of Congress Cataloging-in-Publication Data

Wray, J. Harry.
    Sense and non-sense : American culture and politics / J. Harry Wray.
        p. cm.
    Includes index.
    ISBN 0-13-083343-6 (pbk.)
        1. Political culture—United States—Case studies.   2. United States—Politics and
    government—20th century—Case studies.   I. Title.

JA75.7.W72 2001
306.2'0973—dc21   00-039203

VP, Editorial Director: Laura Pearson
Editorial/production Supervision and Interior Design: Mary Araneo
Prepress and Manufacturing Buyer: Ben Smith
Director of Marketing: Beth Gillett Mejia
Cover Art Director: Jayne Conte
Cover Designer: Bruce Kenselaar
Cover Photo: Siede Preis/PhotoDisc, Inc.

This book was set in 10/12 New Century Schoolbook by
A & A Publishing Services, Inc., and was printed and
bound by Courier Companies, Inc. The cover was printed
by Phoenix Color Corp.

© 2001 by Prentice-Hall, Inc.
A Division of Pearson Education
Upper Saddle River, New Jersey 07458

Printed in the United States of America

10   9   8   7   6   5   4   3   2   1

ISBN 0-13-083343-6

Prentice-Hall International (UK) Limited, *London*
Prentice-Hall of Australia Pty. Limited, *Sydney*
Prentice-Hall Canada Inc., *Toronto*
Prentice-Hall Hispanoamericana, S.A., *Mexico*
Prentice-Hall of India Private Limited, *New Delhi*
Prentice-Hall of Japan, Inc., *Tokyo*
Pearson Education Asia Pte. Ltd., *Singapore*
Editora Prentice-Hall do Brasil, Ltda., *Rio de Janeiro*

for

Judy, Mahli, and John

Contents

Preface

A fundamental task of political science is to shed light on how political systems in various societies work. In pursuit of this goal, one important guiding question is, "How does one account for the distributive decisions that are generated by a political system?" There are a number of ways those interested in the political system of the United States seek to answer this question. One explanatory mode that I believe is underutilized is the assessment of political culture. The intent of this book is therefore to introduce students to the ways that American culture structures the outcomes of political life.

To place the argument of this book in context, it is useful first to identify other ways in which political scientists account for policy outcomes. The kinds of explanation typically used by those seeking to describe American politics may be framed by considering one of the most important domestic policy initiatives in recent years: The Clinton Administration's attempt to establish a comprehensive health care system for the United States. National health care is an interesting political issue, in part because of the wealth of this country, in part because of the significance most of us give to the importance of health to a good life, and in part because the United States stands alone among the industrialized nations of the world in its reluctance to implement a national health care plan.

Perhaps the most common way to answer distributive questions of this sort is to treat each idiosyncratically, without reference to any connections or underlying commonalities among policies. This "case study" approach is useful. Each policy pattern is, after all, complex and to some degree distinctive. Case studies are edifying because they highlight these distinctions. A case study of the attempt by the Clinton Administration's health care initiative might suggest, for example, that it failed for idiosyncratic reasons—because of underlying resentment of Mrs. Clinton's leadership role, inappropriate for a "first lady," or because policy guru Ira Magaziner was politically inept. Or, perhaps Clinton's plan failed simply because it was too complex for average Americans to understand. Each of these possibilities is plausible. As explanations, they are relevant only to health care policy. Mrs. Clinton was far less involved in other policies; other Clinton proposals might have been more straightforward, and so forth.

A second way to understand policy patterns is to look for things that bind them, to consider whether they are part of a larger pattern that reveals important properties of the political system. This approach is also useful. It may miss nuance, but it directs attention to the whole, to theoretical issues. One such explanation locates policy within the matrix of distinctive political institutions. Institutional analysis, for example, might suggest that we do not have national health care because of the uncertainties of this nation's Founders who, living at the dawn of a democratic age, were also fearful of what this age might portend. Health care was doomed by those timid souls who fragmented the political system *precisely* to make political accomplishment difficult. Because the U.S. political system disburses power across an array of institutions, policy accomplishment is problematic. In this case, the Congress, always responsive to a different array of interests than the Presidency, could not be rallied to support Clinton's plan. In this sense, health care failure might well be viewed as simply business as usual.

A differing explanation of this general type ties political outcomes to more fundamental economic forces. Scratch the surface of a given political pattern and one will find the forces of raw economic power at work. Political outcomes are controlled by economic elites. In this understanding, national health care was whipsawed between the Scylla of a media campaign funded by insurance companies and the Charybdis of PAC contributions to financially strapped politicians.

The approach used in this book is to consider policy patterns such as national health care through the prism of political culture. This approach neither argues for the primacy of culture nor gainsays the importance of the other perspectives just described. The forces shaping particular political outcomes are, at some level, unique. And there can be little doubt that both the array of political institutions and economic factors are crucial to political life in this or any other country.

The argument of this book is that the understanding of American politics can also be enhanced by considering the cultural context in which political struggles take place. Policy outcomes are not *merely* random occurrences. They are structured and connected. A fragmented political system makes political accomplishment more difficult, but it does not prevent it. And for all the power it exerts in political life, capitalism in America is quite different from capitalism in Sweden or China. Political outcomes are not completely explained by autonomous economic forces. Capitalist Canada, for example, has a well-established national health care system.

For these reasons, political culture, far less frequently considered in explaining political outcomes, is also important. Policy questions such as national health care are debated and evaluated in a cultural context, and a culture that privileges individualism, competition, and private material acquisition over other versions of reality is politically relevant to policy outcomes. In such a milieu, policies like national health care face an uphill battle.

To recognize the significance of culture in politics is commonplace. Cultures, those shared versions of reality that bind people together, are universal, a fundamental characteristic of human organization. Any society must generate shared symbol systems in order to survive in a world that is indifferently ambiguous. Unproven but common understandings about the nature of reality develop, and these allow for daily discourse and social cohesion. The problems in Bosnia, for example, are fundamentally connected to the inability of its citizens to share some version of reality. In short, no culture, no society. They therefore must be important politically.

It is one thing to recognize the significance of culture abstractly; it is quite another to discuss it in specific terms. For several reasons the subject is daunting, and this may account for the lack of attention to it. Cultures are pervasive and evolving. They cannot be described fully. There is no way to account for all of the cultural nuances relevant to an understanding of American political life, and nowhere to stand to see our culture wholly and clearly. Simultaneously, and ironically, culture is something that, by definition, we are all experts in. Because cultures bind members of a group, their characteristics must be palpable to them. Those who treasure the throne of expertise would be wise to look elsewhere for a subject.

These inherent features of the subject matter give one pause. And yet, because cultures are an essential ingredient for understanding political life, they need to be considered and assessed. This book is not an attempt to discuss the entire U.S. political culture. Rather, I have focused on four characteristics that I believe reverberate powerfully through it.

Even though I have been thinking about American political culture for a number of years, I am sure I don't have it completely right. This is part of the subject's fascination. But I hope I have enough of it right so that this book will stimulate interesting conversations. One of the ways in which cultures evolve into more compelling and useful social "stories" is by bringing them to consciousness and evaluating them.

The eight chapters of this book may be divided into three parts. The first part, comprised of Chapters One and Two, establishes the setting for considering American political culture. Chapter One introduces the concept of culture and explains why cultures are necessary for social life. It also discusses why, even though they are difficult to analyze, cultures are important for political life. Chapter Two establishes a political setting that provides a frame for understanding American political culture. Space is given to considering the meaning of politics and democracy because these concepts recur throughout the book. The bulk of the chapter identifies some political policies and attitudes that are distinctively American.

Chapters Three through Seven comprise the core of the book. These chapters discuss four dominant and distinctive cultural characteristics of U.S. society: individualism, competition, mobility, and materialism. I define each of these concepts, trace their origins and development, identify ways in which they are reinforced and extended in contemporary society, and consider some of their social and political effects.

Chapter Eight returns to some of the questions raised in the initial section of the book. I show how the characteristics that have been considered individually work in concert to contribute to the political curiosities identified in the second chapter. I also argue that these cultural characteristics are increasingly out of sync with everyday life experience and, in consequence, their ability to bind people together—the essential function of a culture—is diminished. I also discuss why they nevertheless remain powerful in contemporary society. The final section of this chapter considers cultural change, leaving open the question of whether such change is likely.

J. Harry Wray

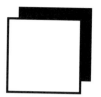

Acknowledgments

I am deeply grateful to colleagues and friends for commenting on early drafts of chapters, and discussing the subject with me. In particular, I wish to thank Larry Bennett, Jim Block, Laura Coats, Terry Lynch, Alan Sroufe, June Sroufe, Wayne Steger, Dale Tobias, Maria Torres, and Judy Wray. Mark and Monica Bennett, Wilma Kwit, Jessica McTigue, and Emily Lander provided valuable research support and technical assistance.

I owe a special debt to Bob Holsworth, with whom I collaborated on an earlier book, *American Politics and Everyday Life*. That work sparked an interest in political culture that continues unabated. Some of the insights on the consumer society contained in that earlier work have been incorporated into this one. While working on this manuscript, I also contributed two chapters to *Politics and Marketing*, Bruce I. Newman, ed. The discussion of politics and democracy in chapter two, and some of the material on television are refinements of ideas appearing first in my chapters in *Politics and Marketing*.

I am grateful to Beth Ann Gillett, former Executive Editor for Political Science and now Director of Marketing at Prentice Hall, for her faith in, and support for, this project. Mary Araneo provided careful and invaluable editorial assistance. I'd like to also thank the following reviewers: Kristen Renwick Monroe, University of California at Irvine; Diana Owen, Georgetown University; and Daniel Shea, Allegheny College.

In many ways, this book was made possible by DePaul University. I wish to thank University faculty and administrators for granting the release time necessary to bring this book to fruition. Margaret Powers and her library research staff, whose competence is matched by their consistent good cheer, helped chase down information and data. Most important, the students who have taken my political culture class through the years have contributed to the development of these ideas and been a major source of inspiration as well. With such students, it is hard not to be optimistic about this nation's future.

Sense and Non-Sense

1

Culture and Politics

As this is being written, a violent thunderstorm blankets Chicago. The storm will provoke varied responses depending upon the particular circumstances of individuals in this community. Some will be pleased that the storm brings with it the water necessary to sustain summer lawns. Others will fret over the possible postponement of the Cubs/Mets baseball game. Still others will regret that they forgot to bring an umbrella to work. The storm will remind some that they live in inferior housing that provides only marginal protection from the elements. Commuters will tune in to radio weather reports to hear if flooding will hamper their exodus from the city. Meaning is conferred depending in part upon the diverse circumstances in which the storm is experienced.

Personal circumstances provide only one source of meaning for the storm, however. There is also a more analytical context in which it is located. Scientifically, we understand storms in a certain way, and this understanding is broadly shared. In this sense, thunderstorms are seen as the result of physical phenomena—a hot air mass colliding with a cooler one in the presence of other conditions. This understanding is regularly ratified on the evening news and is so common that little thought is given to it.

In the mountains of central Malaya live tribes of aboriginal people collectively known as the Semai.[1] They, too, experience periodic thunderstorms, but their understanding of storms' origins is decidedly different. To the Semai, thunderstorms represent violations of the natural order and are mostly the result of human actions. Making too much noise, fooling around with dark-colored objects, and playing with flashing things such as mirrors or dragonflies can attract dark thunder squalls and flashes of lightning. Breaking incest taboos, being cruel to something defenseless, or eating certain combinations of food may bring on thunderstorms as well. In these latter cases, the Semai believe a violation of the social order stimulates a parallel upheaval in the natural world.

To restore order to the natural world, a Semai may engage in rituals to Thunder (a high God). The most common of these rituals involves holding a container in the rain until it is nearly full, then gashing one's shin with a bamboo knife. The penitent then mixes blood with the rain water in the container and casts the liquid into the wind while crying for forgiveness. The Semai believe that, by punishing themselves for violating the natural order, they assuage the anger of Thunder and elicit pity.

The pervasiveness of modern scientific sensibility in our society is such that it is difficult not to regard the Semai understandings with some disdain. Their views seem exotic. We are not likely to be persuaded by the abundant empirical data the Semai could summon to demonstrate that their rituals invariably "cause" the rains to stop. A moment's reflection, however, would reveal that the Semai understanding of thunderstorms is not as strange as it seems at first blush.

While it is probably true that most people in our society are content to define thunderstorms in terms that can be scientifically demonstrated, others are unwilling to do so. Instead, they see various weather patterns as "acts of God," and some see natural catastrophes as divine punishment for sinful human acts. Pat Robertson, a candidate for President and featured speaker at the Republican National Political Convention in 1992, claimed that he and his followers, through prayerful intercession with God, turned Hurricane Gloria away from the eastern seaboard of the United States in 1985.

The point of this discussion is not to determine the "right" way to think about the reasons for thunderstorms, but to underscore a basic property of the human species. The drive for meaning occurs in a world that is inherently complex, ambiguous, and resistant to understanding. Eventually we may come to know things but, given the complexity of circumstances, even certain knowledge is, in reality, tentative.

People once knew, for example, that the world was flat. This knowledge could be demonstrated scientifically, and life was organized around the certainty of this fact. Similarly, Isaac Newton convincingly demonstrated to the eighteenth century European community that the universe was a blended harmony of concordant parts. He compared the universe to a giant clock, operating with precise movements that were in principle knowable. This vision dominated scientific and popular consciousness for two hundred years until physicists such as Albert Einstein, Werner Heisenberg, and Nils Bohr revolutionized our vision of the universe. The disposition to impose order is so ubiquitous, so universal, that it is probably genetically programmed. And it is out of this disposition that cultures grow.

"WHAT A PIECE OF WORK IS MAN!"

A good way to begin considering politics and culture is to think about the nature of that culture-building creature, the human being. This is not the sort of terrain in which social scientists are particularly comfortable. Smaller questions, such as "Which candidate will likely win the November election?" are dealt with more easily. Yet the vast majority of social scientists do recognize that their work inevitably makes assumptions about human nature, even if these are not recognized explicitly. Ideas about what people are like reside in all of us, and these not only shape the work that we do but also influence our behavior in everyday life.

Nevertheless, defining a human being seems to be an act of hubris. If understanding thunderstorms is such a problem, how can we really claim to know what the infinitely more complex human being is like? It is a task that should be approached modestly, tentatively, and with a sense of irony. A few years ago the philosopher Kenneth Burke wrote just such an essay.[2] Writing at a time when there was less sensitivity to gender neutrality in language, he entitled his essay, "Definition of Man."

Burke's definition is offered as a series of clauses, each identifying a distinctively human characteristic. These clauses are followed by paragraphs of lively and evocative reflection. Burke hopes either to persuade us that his definition "fills the bill" or that the reader will be prompted "to decide what should be added, or subtracted, or in some way modified." The following series of clauses are largely taken from Burke's definition. The discussion of these clauses, however, has been written with an eye toward the purposes of this book.

Humans are symbol-using animals. No other creatures come close to humans in their capacity for symbolic representation. The most obvious symbol system is language. In a narrow sense, words are representational. What one sees on this page is not a random splashing of ink. On the contrary, we recognize these ink stains as a tightly managed configuration of letters forming words and sentences which represent something other than the smudges they literally are. Readers have, in turn, learned to interpret these ink smudges in a meaningful manner.

This use of symbols, so integral to human life, is also problematic. Symbols inherently represent things; they are not the things themselves. But because they are so ubiquitous, symbols can be mistaken for the things themselves. Consider U.S. history. It is impossible to "know" the nineteenth century. One can only know about it, and then only in the most abbreviated, representational way. In a very real sense, history *becomes* its symbolic form. In consciousness, it *is* what one learns about it.

Because history is representational, the struggle over what to include in a high school civics text, for example, often assumes an ideological hue. Recently a group of prominent historians and history teachers, under the aegis of a grant from the federal government, engaged in an intensive effort to generate voluntary national standards for high school U.S. history courses. One conclusion of the committee was that the role of social movements had been regularly undervalued in history texts, and therefore they proposed standards giving these social movements more prominence. The group labored mightily to generate a consensual view of history, but the standards were assailed from a variety of perspectives. Criticism from Rush Limbaugh and other conservatives largely revolved around the conviction that famous political leaders like George Washington were not mentioned often enough, and that patriotism was therefore undermined.[3] Such disputes have contemporary political significance. Is political change primarily a function of great leaders or of mass struggle by ordinary people? The way the past is conceived influences the sense of possibility in the present.

Although the symbol-using characteristic of humans is most obvious in language, it extends to vast areas of everyday social life. Can anyone doubt that the trial of O.J. Simpson for allegedly murdering his wife was so dramatic and compelling precisely because of what he symbolized to various groups? Similarly, a young world traveler, away from home for the first time, could easily be uncomfortable about being in Budapest because of an inability to access the symbol system in use there. Just as she is on the verge of coming unglued, she sees in the distance a beautiful pair of Golden Arches and is immediately filled with a sense of well-being and tranquility. Symbols imparting a sense of the familiar restore the traveler to a settled state.

Inventors of the negative. By this phrase Burke does not mean to imply that humans are negative in the ordinary sense that there is much that they don't like. Rather, he is calling attention to the fact that, in nature, there are no negatives as such. Everything simply is what it is, as it is. Negative thinking is the capacity that allows people to imagine things being *other* than what they are. Without it, symbol-usage would be impossible. In order to use words at all, humans must know that they are *not* the things they stand for. Negative thinking unleashes considerable creative or destructive power. A settler, coming to a pristine meadow, can imagine the negation of that meadow and thus erects a house in the middle of it. A group of entrepreneurs in Minnesota can imagine the existence of Mall America. Others can imagine its demise. Bill Clinton can, at the age of seventeen, imagine himself in the White House.

The capacity for negative thought is portentous for the character of social life. It makes conversation possible. One can consider an idea to be wrong, or suggestive, or interesting, any one of which implies the negation of the idea. Negative thinking allows for the possibility of choice and rebellion. It is inextricably tied to notions of freedom. Adolescence, during which the phrase "I am" comes to be taken very seriously, begins with the assertion, "I am not." Because it does not accept the given world as inevitable, negative thinking makes it possible to set standards of moral conduct. Martin Luther King, Jr., dreamed of a world in which the absence of racism was a reality. Adolf Hitler had a dream of a rather different sort.

Separated from their natural condition by instruments of their own making. Human beings do not simply exist passively in the world. They act on and in their environments, reshaping them to serve various ends. In the process of this transformation, humans are themselves transformed. Humans are never *merely* creatures of their environment, but they are always *somewhat* so. This clause also recognizes that humans are inherently cultural beings. The eminent anthropologist Clifford Geertz[4] believes that the acquisition of culture is inextricably intertwined with biological evolution. "By submitting himself to governance by symbolically mediated programs . . . man determined, if unwittingly, the culminating stages of his own biological destiny. Quite literally, though quite inadvertently, he created himself."

Humans in every society have acted on settings to make them more serviceable to the ends of that society. Other actions on the environment have unintended consequences. It has always been thus. When archaeologists attempt to determine whether fossilized remains are of human origin or of some other primate, one of the telling clues they look for is the existence of tools at the site.

This re-creation of the environment has consequences for those who live in it, affecting their perspectives and senses of reality. New environments impose new imperatives. Teenagers in a wealthy suburb have a very different set of possibilities and worries than do their counterparts in a public housing project. In the former environment, much is taken for granted. Food, clothing, protection are given. Life seems to be very good, which is why events like the shootings at Columbine are so shocking. Kids in wealthy suburbs do face serious problems, however. Not the least of these is—in this success-oriented culture—outperforming parents, who have themselves been pretty successful. Their environment imparts a different sensibility than does the environment of public housing projects, where very different things are taken for granted. In his chronicle of life in the projects, Alex Kotlowitz notes that thinking about the future is much more tentative.[5] Children tend to preface statements about the future with the phrase "If I grow up . . ." In such an environment, "making it" may be defined by simply surviving.

And moved by a sense of order. One of the paradoxes in Burke's definition of human beings is that while, on one hand, they are inventors of the negative, actively involved in changing their environments, they also have a need for order. This last phrase implies predictability and seems to contradict the earlier characteristics. It does, but so what? Many creative thinkers recognize that much of the dynamic of human existence revolves around polarities: the yin and the yang, the dialectic of Plato, Hegel, and Marx, good versus evil, the individual and the community, the sperm and the egg, labor and rest. Truthfulness is a more important standard than consistency, and Burke's definition seems to be faithful to human experience and behavior.

As we shall see, U.S. society places great value on individualism and originality, so much so that it is easy to forget how important orderliness and predictability are, even in this culture. Order animates social life. People regularly expect the newspaper to be there in the morning, Richard Simmons to be unctuous, friends to remain friends, classes to begin and end at specified times, and the Red Sox not to win a World Series. The success of franchise food chains suggests that serving bad food can be profitable so long as the food is *predictably* bad. Although novelty may be intriguing, most of the time people seem disposed to impose a sense of order onto novel situations. Novelty is often greeted with nervous laughter, while minds race to locate it in some pattern of previous experience. Such laughter grows not out of humor, but out of fear—the fear of being outside an ordering context in which the rules are familiar.

PEOPLE AND CULTURE

Burke's definition of human beings may not account for all the important and distinctive properties of our species. It does, however, help us understand culture. Cultures grow out of the basic human characteristics that Burke identifies, in combination with the predisposition of our species for living together.

In political science, Aristotle has provided the most famous recognition of this predisposition with his dictum "Man is a political animal." For the Greeks in Aristotle's time, the polis represented much more than what is meant by "the political arena" today. Contemporary citizens think of the modern political arena as something that can be easily ignored. In fact, the phrase "That's politics" is often used to describe a set of attitudes and behaviors that is morally beneath any right-thinking person. Today most U.S. citizens do not even vote regularly. It hardly seems that politics is part of human nature.

Aristotle's use of the term "politics" differs from modern usage in that it identifies a public aspect of human existence, a dimension of life that is necessarily lived in common with others. Thus, some modern interpreters of Aristotle find the term "social animal" closer to what Aristotle had in mind by his use of the term. Wherever one finds people, one finds them in groups. The occasional recluse may be considered a saint or a quack, but these very characterizations indicate how oddly such a lifestyle is regarded.

Certainly communities can stifle individual development, but to conclude that life is a struggle *against* community is to miss the essence of humanity. Far from existing in opposition to the self, the community is necessary to allow for the fullest development of the self. Outside a community, the self is inevitably stunted. If moral thought—the capacity to think from the perspective of another, or to imagine how another feels—represents the highest stage of personal development, as Jean Piaget[6] argues, achieving this stage is impossible outside the bonds of community. Morality is a guide to *social* conduct. No one can be moral in isolation. Community is in turn impossible without some mechanism, such as politics, to resolve disputes and claims.

As it is used in this book, the word "culture" means a *shared symbol system, linking members of a group to each other and to history, thus providing them with an identity.* No claim is made that this is a perfect definition. It differs somewhat from some definitions used by political scientists.[7] Nevertheless, this definition is useful because it calls attention to several essential features of culture.

First, the definition indicates that cultures are created out of the human capacity for symbol usage. The real world is extraordinarily rich and complex. In Sheldon Wolin's phrase,[8] facts are multifaceted, having dimensions that are variously accessible. In order to make our way in the world, we must construct simplifying symbols of the things encountered. Cultures are patterns of these constructs. In this sense, all seeing is what Abraham Kaplan calls "seeing-that." "Give a child a hammer," Kaplan writes, "and he will soon discover that all the world is a nail."[9] Hence, when the Semai encounter a thunderstorm they "see-that" the gods are angry. To paraphrase Geertz, humans are animals suspended in webs of significance which they themselves have spun.[10] Culture *is* that webbing. If we began each day anew, if all contact and experience were interminably unique, social life would be impossible. Jarring as it is, we know that the clock radio in the morning is a mechanical device prodding us awake, not a stranger standing at the foot of our bed. The voice on the radio symbolizes not a mortal threat but the (perhaps only slightly less daunting) need to rise and face the day.

Second, cultures require that the patterns of symbols simplifying the world be consciously shared. They do not need to be universally shared in the society, but they do need to be shared in some coherent fashion. This does not imply that people hold no patterns of beliefs that are in some sense unique; only that, insofar as they are unique, these are not cultural. Some ways of seeing are more broadly shared than others, and within a given political boundary, alternative ways of seeing may be shared by competing groups, giving rise to such concepts as dominant, sub-, counter-, and multi-cultures. At this point we must keep in mind that cultures involve symbol systems shared by members of a group.

Living among a group of people, but outside their shared symbol system, can be traumatic, for it is the act of sharing that binds group members, providing the essential glue of the community. This sharing links people not only to each other but also to the past and, therefore, generates a sense of place and identity. Thus, although cultures arise from the human inclination to act on the world, they also appeal to the longing for a sense of order that Burke sees as characteristically human.

Since they are collective ways of "seeing-that," cultures provide a comfort zone for daily life. The patterns become quite familiar and are regular parts of everyday experience. Operating within these patterns allows one to get through life's daily chores with a minimum of stress. If it is shared broadly enough, a common *view* of reality often comes to be accepted as reality itself. In Alabama, for example, the importance of the Alabama-Auburn football game is accepted as a given. An outsider, stopping at a gas station, or attending virtually any type of social gathering in that state, can gain a modicum of acceptance merely by raising a question about an upcoming or past game. A New Yorker, convinced of her sophistication, might raise the point that the game *really* doesn't matter at all, but an Alabaman knows different. On game days, the business of the state stops. Other rituals, such as weddings or funerals, are organized, if possible, so as not to conflict with the game. Men, women, and children weep over the outcome, locate it in historic context, and begin to develop scenarios for the next game. In Alabama, the game *really does* matter. People in that state can tell you where they were when they learned of the death of legendary Alabama coach Bear Bryant, just as other older Americans can for the assassination of President John Kennedy.

Depending upon the importance of the shared norm, an outsider may be regarded by members of the group as eccentric, insane, evil, or even not fully human. The outsider is the other, the one who is not part of the group. It is possible for outsiders to thrive on lower levels of animosity. Some may enjoy being regarded as eccentric, for example. Unless one has established a strong identity with another group, however, marginalization is usually a source of pain and anxiety.

It is not uncommon, even in a country such as the United States where many norms are broadly shared, for people to feel excluded by cultural nuances. The high school "crowds," the romance with someone from an "other" group, visiting an unfamiliar part of the city or state, stepping onto a college campus for the first time—any of these experiences can cause anxiety. Because the rules of membership and symbolic meaning are not known, the outsider feels excluded. Ralph Ellison's *Invisible Man*, one of the works that stimulated the civil rights movement in the fifties, provides a riveting example of the role of race in keeping people in the category of the "other." For Ellison, the most tragic legacy of racism in the United States was that it rendered African-Americans invisible, not to each other, of course, but to those in the dominant culture. This theme has been reiterated by many African-American critics of the society.

The influential historian Oswald Spengler once defined culture as "the personality of a nation." Personalities are properties of individuals; cultures are properties of social collectives. Spengler interposes the individual and the collective. He believed that culture is, at the collective level, what personality is at the individual level. There are some problems with this definition which make it ultimately inadequate, but using "personality" as a metaphor for "culture" does call attention to characteristics that the two concepts share.

Like personalities, cultures have structure. Personalities are stable and they endure. When one thinks of another person as a jerk, for example, one expects a certain amount of stability in that representation. The assumption is that the person was a jerk yesterday and will be so tomorrow. Because it is a characteristic of personality, one is not surprised by jerkish behavior. Were it otherwise, one might ask, "Why are you behaving like (as if you were) a jerk?" Cultures are similar. One expects, and depends upon, stability in the shared symbol systems. Without this stability the group linkage and identity that cultures provide would be impossible.

While personalities endure, however, they also evolve. They have structure, but they are not impervious to experience and growth. Some jerks become rather decent people and some rather decent people become jerks. When first confronted with an evolving personality, one might be justifiably skeptical. One might think, "Strange. That jerk acted like a decent person today." If the newer behaviors persist, one eventually readjusts the assessment of personality. So it is with cultures. They have structure, but they are not ossified. The culture of the United States today, whatever it may be, is very different from the culture of 1900.

There is an additional similarity between cultures and personalities. Developmental psychologists[11] recognize that the evolution and growth of personality is not random. Rather, it is patterned, and integrally connected to what has previously existed. This does not necessarily mean that growth is predictable. The manner in which an individual resolves issues at a given developmental stage may be quite difficult to anticipate. Patterns become more obvious once issues have been resolved. So it is with cultures. Standing at the threshold of the twenty-first century, one can look back at the last hundred years of U.S. cultural history and observe developmental patterns. Our cultural growth has not been random. It has proceeded on the basis of assimilation and accommodation. Anticipating the details of these developmental patterns in 1900, however, would have been impossible.

As it is used in this book, culture differs from a second meaning frequently given to it in our society.[12] In this second sense, culture is frequently used as a means of evaluation, not of description. Culture reflects that which is remarkable in human achievement, a set of standards that helps to distinguish the forward march of civilization. This use should be quite familiar. Thinking of "cultural events" characteristically draws attention to the fine arts—an opera, a poetry reading, or a Native American folk dance. In this sense culture is something to be obtained, not something inherent in everyday social life. This common use of the term is not the way culture is used in this book. As used here, culture is experienced daily, often subconsciously, and is not readily turned on or off.

CULTURE AND DIVERSITY

It is one thing to describe culture as a concept. It is something else to identify and describe a particular culture existing in the real world. The idea of culture is quite plausible, as it resonates with personal experience. We recognize that people share assumptions about the way the world is, that these assumptions are durable and that they help to define those who share the assumptions. Given the rich texture of the world, we can easily see that without shared assumptions life would be difficult indeed. The problem comes in seeking to identify and isolate particular cultural patterns in an actual society. For any given society it is not easy to isolate what is actually shared, or which of the things that are shared deserve special attention. Such efforts are often rife with controversy. Although the fact of culture seems indisputable, its substance remains evanescent.

Early cultural anthropologists tended to ascribe uniform cultural characteristics to very large groups of people. Such descriptions were made easier by a lack of knowledge of another society (people seem less complex when they are not known intimately), racism, and intellectual arrogance. While anthropologists certainly increased our knowledge of "primitive" societies by their studies of them, summary judgments, especially as these studies were distilled by popular media, were often too easily arrived at. Some academics were prone to sweeping assessments about "The German National Character" and "The International Jew." John Higham's[13] study of American nativism reveals a marked proclivity for such easy generalization, not only among common folk, but also in respected academic circles. Characteristics were ascribed to what were considered, at the beginning of the twentieth century, the different races of European peoples. In this environment, Spengler's definition of culture as the "personality of a nation" could seem entirely appropriate.

Such ideas have been seriously eroded by later scholarship. On one hand, there do seem to be broad differences between various living groups. On the other hand, the more familiar one is with a particular living group, the more subtle and nuanced the belief patterns seem to be. Fresh from a first visit to England, one may be full of declaratory statements that begin with the words, "The British . . ." Return trips, however, will bring more complexity to one's initial visions of that society.

To think of a national culture for the United States is especially daunting. More immigrants come to this country annually than to all other nations of the world combined. Surely they bring with them a diverse array of ideas about the nature of reality. Attempts to sustain a particular vision of national character may be little more than thinly-veiled efforts to sustain the dominance of a particular group. Higham shows that this was a powerful motivation a hundred years ago. The more pessimistic nativists wanted to halt altogether the tide of immigrants from southern and central Europe because they felt these new immigrants would contaminate the "race," which they saw as coming from northern Europe. The more hopeful nativists believed that institutions such as public schools would transform these immigrants and instill the "correct" American values in them. They expected the melting pot to produce an acceptably American alchemy.

Both the recognition that images of culture can simply be the product of power plays and increased analytical sophistication have contributed to the rise of the idea of multiculturalism in the United States. Proponents of multiculturalism hold that different groups in the society have differing perspectives and differing shared value systems, that each of these systems has equal moral standing and all are worth studying and sustaining. The metaphor of a melting pot is sometimes supplanted by that of a mosaic, wherein individual, discrete tiles representing the cultures of different social groups sit in combination to form a large picture.

Multiculturalism has had a powerful and positive impact on those interested in questions of culture. It has made us more sensitive to nuance, more cautious about generalization, more respecting of difference. There is greater recognition of the various ways symbols might resonate through a community. And there is increasing awareness that various systems of shared symbols exist in different pockets of society.

Beginning a sporting event with the national anthem is a well-known American tradition. This moment of symbol-sharing is cultural. In an earlier time, students of U.S. culture might have seen it as a moment when diverse citizens put aside petty differences to express a higher loyalty and connection to the nation. There is undoubtedly some truth in this. Some citizens surely attach precisely this meaning to the ritual. In a complex culture, however, such an image does not represent the whole truth.

In everyday experience, the meaning of this shared moment varies. A few grizzled hippies in the crowd may recall a time when meaning was gleaned through defying official authority and refuse to stand or remove their hats. Others may think about how little of the promise of the American Dream they have experienced. An athlete, posing reverently on the sideline for the television cameras, may think about how to parlay this moment into a richer advertising contract. Still others, watching from their living rooms, see an opportunity to raid the refrigerator. Chicago Blackhawks hockey fans are boisterous throughout the anthem, regarding it as a time to psyche up for the ensuing mayhem. The meaning of the anthem also differs depending upon whether it is sung by the West Point Cadet Chorus, Aretha Franklin, or Roseanne. Sometimes the anthem is used, not for integration, but to establish separateness. In a World Series, for example, competing cities use contrasting renditions to typify their distinctiveness. Thus we have New York, home of Robert Merrill and the Lyric Opera, battling Los Angeles, the land of Linda Ronstadt and laid-back pop.

One of the contributions of multiculturalism is that it makes us more sensitive to the kinds of realities presented by this example. Easy generalizations can obscure underlying truth. But limiting the study of culture to the values generated by various groups in a society is also problematic, for these are unlikely to yield a satisfactory picture of the whole, as the mosaic metaphor suggests. In any given society, differing groups can generate distinctive cultural patterns. Which of these ought to be studied? Which comprise the tiles of the mosaic? The answer should not be merely a function of political power. That was the basis for the attack on older, singular cultural visions in the first place. Some groups, perhaps because of their cohesion, or language differences, or because they have been excluded from full participation in the larger society, might be fairly easy to identify. But while the culture generated by such groups is important and worthy of study, to think of it as a discrete tile in a larger mosaic is unsatisfying.

Spanish-speaking Americans comprise the fastest growing ethnic group in the United States. Should "Latino" culture comprise a tile in the national mosaic? Perhaps. But a Puerto Rican, a Columbian, and a Mexican might feel discomfort to find their cultures fused in only one tile. A Cuban entrepreneur, who comes to Miami after the government has taken over his successful business in Cuba, may have more in common with Donald Trump than he has with an immigrant Mexican farm worker.

We have become increasingly aware in recent years of the distinctive experiences of women and men in U.S. society. Many would argue that women deserve their own tile in the great American mosaic. Surely the distinctive gender experiences hold for other societies as well. Should we therefore be content with a tile for Mexicans, or should there be one each for Mexican men and women? What about Mexican women college graduates? Married Mexican women college graduates? Married working Mexican women college graduates with children? It can be reasonably claimed that each of these situations—and we have hardly scratched the surface of possibility—generate a particular community with a distinctive vision of reality. Each may be worthy of study in its own right. In terms of describing the larger society, however, such iterations are problematic. It is easy to see where the legitimate claims of multiculturalism begin; it is more difficult to see where they end. It places one on a slippery slope where, at the bottom, the idea of culture dissolves into a matter of personal identity.

The mosaic metaphor also implies, as Gertrude Stein said about Oakland, that there is no there, there. Tiles in a mosaic are discrete, and are unaffected even by tiles to which they are adjacent. This is an implausible representation of any social order. When immigrants arrive in this country they bring with them some image of what the United States is like. A Vietnamese immigrant may intend to reside in a Vietnamese community in Garden Grove, California, but he knows he is not going to another Vietnam, and he probably would not want to.

Furthermore, a member of any group in this society inevitably interacts with those outside the group. The effects of this *inter*action are reciprocal, running in both directions. Any second generation Mexican-American who returns to Mexico for a visit knows immediately that she is no longer simply a Mexican. She will certainly recognize similarities in herself and her Mexican friends, but she will doubtless be just as struck by the differences. This does not mean that she has become a Norteamericana, although that is how she may be regarded by her Mexican friends. She will feel that she is somewhere between these two cultures.[14] Perhaps a tile should be created for her, but what of her children, whose connections to Mexico will be more distant but probably not eroded altogether?

The metaphor of a mosaic emerged as a reaction to the melting pot. The melting pot metaphor implied a process wherein past identities were transformed into some common, predetermined view of Americanism, just as metals in a melting pot are blended. This view of Americanism, however, seemed to come from the minds of the analysts, not from the pot itself. Perhaps a more appropriate metaphorical pot for a culture is a cooking pot. All metaphors have their limitations, but if one thinks of a cooking pot in action, it may not be such a poor one for the way cultures work. As vegetables are added to the base of a stew, for example, the character of the stew is altered. Over time, the vegetables will begin to dissolve into the stew, some more quickly than others. Eventually some of the vegetables may dissolve completely, but what has really happened? The dissolved vegetables have not disappeared, they have simply become more integrated into the larger mixture. An exchange has occurred. They have been affected by the larger broth, but they have also affected it. In the assimilation of the vegetables, the character of the broth itself is altered.

Swedish anthropologist Ulf Hannerz has written about what he terms "cultural complexity."[15] He recognizes that cultures are part of the process of "making sense" of the world, of imposing meaning because atomized comprehension of the rich possibilities would make social life impossible. Thus, culture construction is the creation of "publicly meaningful forms."

Hannerz identifies three interrelated dimensions of culture: 1) ideas and modes of thought—the array of concepts and values which people carry together in their minds; 2) forms of externalization—or how this meaning is made public; and 3) social distribution—the way in which this collective cultural inventory is spread over the population. This third dimension is an especially powerful addition to the understanding of culture. His analysis calls attention to an important fact, and one that fits comfortably with Kenneth Burke's previously discussed definition of human beings. While there is probably an element of coercion in the acceptance of cultural norms, cultures are not *merely* imposed. Part of the price for life in community is the acceptance of particular ways of seeing. On the other hand, as Burke recognized, humans are more than herd animals. They are creative, imaginative, playful. Some, for whatever reason, are more restless than others. Most important, in complex cultures especially (by this term Hannerz refers to post–modern industrial cultures) the need for group identity can be satisfied in diverse ways.

Thus, in the 1950s the Beats, sharp critics of modern American culture and society, lived together in places like Greenwich Village in New York City and North Beach in San Francisco sharing their ideas with each other in coffee houses and at poetry readings. To most Americans, they seemed to be anti-social (anti-cultural?) but they were anything but that. For one thing, they were drawing upon the powerful strain of individualism that exists in the larger American culture. Moreover, the bonds of community they established and the norms they shared were clearly observable. These simply differed somewhat from those of the larger community. Even libertarians, who profess great disdain for ideas of community, meet in Ayn Rand societies and form political parties to declaim against collectivist apostasy.

The paradox of culture is that it seems to be simultaneously structure and process, static and evolving. Hannerz finds a river to be a useful metaphor. Looked upon from one vantage point, say from an airplane, a mighty river seems permanent and unchanging. But at the same time, "You cannot ever step into the same river twice" for it is always moving, and it is through this movement that the river adapts and achieves its durability.

How a culture adapts and evolves is often odd and unpredictable. The Beats might have remained in their tiny urban enclaves, isolated and giving solace to one another, an irrelevant backwater in our cultural river. But, through an unpredictable string of events, this was not to be. In 1955 Allen Ginsberg reads his poem *Howl* to a rapt audience of compatriots at the Six Gallery in San Francisco. For some reason the event receives a flicker of attention from the mainstream media. The government subsequently seeks to ban the importation of *Howl*, which had been published by a British press. Protest. More attention. Soon, *Time* and *Newsweek* do pieces on the Beats, now labeled Beatniks. In odd ways, the Beat ethos begins to seep into mainstream culture. Some college students read their books. Beatnik characters emerge in lame TV sitcoms. Their language is co-opted. Some of the emerging sixties radicals take the Beats especially seriously. In 1963 *Time* and *Newsweek*, two guardians of official culture, carry pieces in which that year's college graduating class is described as one of the happiest, most tranquil groups ever. That tranquility was short-lived. Two years later, in one of the notable events of that notable decade, Ginsberg and a few of his youthful followers seek, through chanting, to levitate the Pentagon and are assaulted by government troops. The backwater eddy of Beat culture eventually contributes (other things do also, of course) to the culture storm of the sixties. The ripples generated by the Beats are felt even today as contemporary college students devour Beat literature and MTV introduces icons Ginsberg and William Burroughs to its young audience.

ENTER POLITICS

This discussion indicates why culture is integrally connected to politics. If cultures are ordered and shared ways of seeing, they will necessarily have a vital impact on the character of political life. Ideas about political possibility that make perfect sense in one society seem quixotic in another society. Notions of family may exemplify the way culture connects to politics. In recent years, American politicians of various ideologies have fallen over each other in their efforts to convince the public of their support for the family. One would think, given the florid rhetoric of political leaders, that no society is more devoted to the preservation of the family than is our own. Passing a Family Leave Bill, however, was for years a matter of great controversy. The proposed bill would allow a parent of a newborn child to take up to sixteen weeks of leave without pay from most work places—small businesses were excluded—without fear of being fired by their employers. An early version of this bill was vetoed by President Bush, but it was later passed and signed into law by President Clinton.

In contrast, Sweden has long given new parents various options. In that country, either parent may take up to a year off, *with* eighty percent of pay, to care for a newborn child. Or, they may reduce their work days to five hours over several years of early childhood and still receive full pay. Given both the political rhetoric and the abundant data from studies of developmental psychology suggesting the importance of attachment during early childhood, one might assume U.S. policy would be more "family friendly." How does one explain public policy in this area?

The most common explanation typically offered for policies like family leave emphasizes notions of power and its distribution. One might understand U.S. family leave policy, for example, by seeing that powerful economic interests oppose a comparatively generous leave policy. Big business simply uses this power to stifle any significant movement in the direction of subsidized leave. This explanation doubtless contains elements of truth, but it does not capture the whole truth. In the first place it begs the question of why economic interests have been allowed to gather so much political power in this society, but not in Sweden. Second, it does not indicate why explanations and rationales in support of this policy make sense to Americans, while the policy of Sweden seems like an extravagance. Each of these questions can be addressed, and our understanding of the political process enhanced, by a consideration of how culture affects politics.

Knowledge about culture in a given society helps illuminate the character of politics in that society. However, cultural analysis is inherently messy and treacherous. The influence of culture begins at conception, as ritualized patterns of child-bearing set in, gathers momentum with birth, and spins dizzily toward what has been called "the American way of death."[16] Culture is constantly swirling around and through people, including cultural analysts. There is no place to stand to see it objectively. Complicating this is the previously discussed fact that cultures are richly layered. There is no single cultural pattern that engulfs everyone in U.S. society. Each of us belongs to distinctive groups generating values that may conflict with dominant cultural patterns. Competing ways of seeing are layered throughout the society.

Given cultural complexity, it is not surprising that there is not a large body of literature on American politics and culture. Most work on political culture has focused on other societies. When studying other societies, political scientists easily see the importance of cultures in shaping social attitudes. Much of the work done in this area has been interesting and important. However it is made easier by the fact that distance makes that culture (to use Hannerz's river metaphor) seem more like a frozen line. It is easier to draw, although the result is a necessarily crude depiction of the river. Trying to reproduce the shape of the river while standing in it is much more problematic.

Those who do write about American political culture usually focus upon patterns of ideas existing in the political realm.[17] The details of these patterns are typically gleaned from surveys. Characteristically the ideas are broad, which supposedly makes them cultural. Usually they are spindly things, with rickety struts that do not seem to be supporting much at all. Why is one pattern of reported beliefs cultural and another not? An American Government text may have a chapter on political culture, although most do not. When there is such a chapter, it is usually self-contained—seemingly irrelevant to subsequent chapters on the presidency, Congress, elections, and so forth. The whole point of culture—that it shapes values and attitudes and is therefore integral to the political process—is often missed.

What follows is an invitation to a conversation about important characteristics of American culture and politics. In her evocative study showing how urban land-use patterns both shape and reflect cultural norms, Constance Perin wrote, "I claim not much more than a partial glimmering of the cultural elements with which Americans construct social order."[18] Given the complexity of the topic, such modesty seems entirely appropriate. And yet, *because* culture is politically significant, it deserves attention. My hope is to stimulate thought and reflection about the phenomena that influence the way Americans tend to "see" in political life. Any consideration of this subject is necessarily selective. To say anything at all about politics and culture, one must limit what one says and establish priorities. There will doubtless be disagreement over whether the things selected for attention are the most important, whether the argument is sustained, whether the political consequences of the culture that are identified in fact follow, and so forth. As Clifford Geertz once observed:

> Cultural analysis is intrinsically incomplete. And, worse than that, the more deeply it goes the less complete it is. It is a strange science whose most telling assertions are its most tremulously based, in which to get somewhere with the matter at hand is to intensify the suspicion, both your own and that of others, that you are not quite getting it right.[19]

The work of anthropologists like Geertz and Hannerz, the rise of multiculturalism in the university, and common sense all suggest that there are multiple ways of viewing the world, particularly so in a society as diverse as our own. This complexity encourages avoiding the topic. The task before us is at least marginally simplified by the fact that, although there are multiple ways of viewing the world in any society, not all of them are politically equal. Power is not evenly distributed. Some ideas and values are therefore going to receive more attention, promotion, and extension and are more likely to become the settled or dominant view of reality.

Writing from the Italian prison in which he had been placed by the regime of Benito Mussolini, social theorist Antonio Gramsci developed and elaborated the concept of hegemony.[20] Gramsci recognized two ways in which societies were controlled by elite groups: domination and consent. Domination was characteristic of older social orders. People were obedient to kings because they feared the consequences of disobedience. Domination is costly, however, as it relies on the eternal vigilance of political elites. As a consequence, Gramsci believed modern social orders were moving toward consent as a form of control. But consent did not necessarily imply the happy state of affairs envisioned by the liberal political philosopher John Locke.

"Consent" implies that something is freely given, but Gramsci foresaw the possibility of consent being manipulated. He developed this insight through the concept of hegemony. Hegemony exists when a world view held by a dominant social class is disseminated by social agencies such as schools and the mass media, and is internalized by ordinary people. This world view does not appear as an imposed ideology; rather, it so deeply saturates collective consciousness that it appears as common sense. When these efforts by the ruling class to universalize their own belief systems are successful, people in effect consent to what Gramsci sees as their own exploitation and misery.

One need not embrace the details of Gramsci's general theory to recognize that this kind of thing goes on all the time. Individuals and groups seek to extend their power by determining the kinds of issues that are raised in the political arena, and the ways in which they are discussed. One way to do this is through the perpetuation and extension of certain cultural ideas.

In this book, I have tried to select cultural characteristics important to the political life of this nation. This does not mean that these patterns of ideas are better than those held by others in the society. The point is to show that these shared symbol systems are deeply held, that they have grown out of our historical experience as that experience has been represented to us, and that, although they are prior to politics, they enter the political realm as they often establish what Noam Chomsky has called "the bounds of thinkable thought." They also may be reinforced and extended by the political process itself.

Cultures are not right or wrong. They simply are. One cannot prove whether Americans or Swedes have the correct values with respect to family leave. But since cultures are always evolving even as they provide structure, thinking about the collective assumptions Americans tend to bring to politics will not only generate better understanding of the American political system, but may also help us to participate in directing the course of that evolution. The paradox of culture is that, although human beings are shaped by it, they are also its creators.

As we look around the world, we can see that the varieties of actual human experience are extraordinarily rich. The possibilities seem limitless. Just as our ancestors one hundred years ago could not have imagined what America in 2000 would have been like, who can say what the year 2100 will hold? Certainly it will be connected to the present somehow, but the manner of that connection is obscure. As cultural animals, we create the symbol systems that bind us and define reality. Our future thus depends upon the choices we make and the possibilities we can imagine.

NOTES

1. Dentan, Robert Dentan, *The Semai*, Fort Worth, TX: Holt, Rinehart and Winston, Inc., 1968.
2. *"Definition of Man,"* Kenneth Burke, *Hudson Review* Vol. XVI, no. 4, Winter (1963–64).
3. Gary B. Nash, Charlotte Crabtree, Ross E. Dunn, *History on Trial*, New York: A. A. Knopf, 1995.

4. Clifford Geertz, *The Interpretation of Cultures*, New York: Basic Books, 1973, p.48.

5. Alex Kotlowitz, *There Are No Children Here*, New York: Anchor, 1991.

6. Jean Piaget, *The Moral Judgment of the Child*, New York: The Free Press, 1965. Piaget is generally recognized as the founder of developmental psychology.

7. Gabriel Almond and Sidney Verba have generated the most broadly used definition of culture. See their book, *The Civic Culture Revisited*. New York: Little Brown, 1980. Stephen Chilton has provided a useful analysis of the enduring problems in defining political culture, and pointed to useful directions in "Defining Political Culture," *Western Political Quarterly*, September, 1988.

8. See Sheldon Wolin, "Paradigms and Political Theories," in P. King and B. Parekh, *Politics and Experience*, London: Cambridge University Press, 1968.

9. Abraham Kaplan, *The Conduct of Inquiry*, San Francisco: Chandler Press, 1964, Ch. 10.

10. Clifford Geertz, *op. cit.*, p. 5.

11. For a cogent summary of the developmental perspective in psychology, see *Child Development*, L. Alan Sroufe and Richard G. Cooper, New York: Alfred A. Knopf, 2nd ed., 1993.

12. Chris Jencks has written an excellent summary of how the concept of culture has been used historically and the various philosophical skirmishes over how it is properly used: *Culture*, London: Routledge, 1993.

13. John Higham, *Strangers in the Land*. New York: Athenium, 1963.

14. For an interesting discussion of this topic, see Maria de Los Angeles Torres, "Crossing Theoretical Borders: Transnational Political and Cultural Identities," a paper delivered at the Latin American Studies Association Meetings, April 1997, Guadalajara, Mexico.

15. Ulf Hannerz, *Cultural Complexity*. New York: Columbia University Press, 1992.

16. Jessica Mitford, *The American Way of Death*. New York: Simon & Schuster, 1963.

17. Herbert McCloskey and John Zaller, *The American Ethos*, Cambridge: Harvard University Press, 1984, Oliver Woshinsky, *Culture and Politics*, Upper Saddle River, NJ: Prentice Hall, 1995, and Ron Englehart, "The Renaissance of Political Culture," *American Political Science Review*, Vol. 82, No. 4, December 1988 are good representations of the work done by political scientists in the area of political culture.

18. Constance Perin, *Everything In Its Place*, Princeton, NJ: Princeton University Press, 1977, pp.5–6.

19. Quoted in Jencks, *op. cit.*, p.29.

20. Antonio Gramsci, *Selections from Prison Notebooks*. New York: International Publishers, 1971.

2

Political Curiosities

The United States shares numerous political characteristics with other western, industrialized democracies. In these countries, citizens participate in the process of politics, some social provision is made for those in need, structures are established for national defense, and so forth. Despite such similarities, these systems are not isomorphic. Each has patterns of politics distinguishing them from other, similar nations. Within a political system, these patterns may seem quite "normal" and are not necessarily even noticed. From outside that political system however, the patterns are more noticeable, even curious, to the observer.

A consideration of American "curiosities" will provide insight into the political culture. As shared patterns of values, cultures are necessarily somewhat abstract. They can be made more tangible by considering clearly observable and distinctive political phenomena. These "political curiosities" provide a grounding, a beginning point from which one may more easily move toward the culture that contributes to the observed phenomena. Because this book is an attempt to broaden discussions about how politics works in America, I will first clarify how I use the terms "politics" and "democracy."

POLITICS AND DEMOCRACY

When asked to define the term "politics," most Americans describe a form of tactical behavior that they consider at least slightly illicit and often thoroughly corrupt. "Office politics," for example, is conniving behavior in the workplace. "A political decision" suggests an unsavory desertion of principle in the interests of expedience, and a "political person" is one who constantly calibrates decisions according to narrowly perceived self-interest. The connection of the term "politics" to questionable private behavior indicates how people feel about the public realm. Politics is something conscientious and right-thinking people ought to avoid, and a politician is one who exists just a little closer to the primal ooze than the rest of us, in the nether region shared with pimps, tobacco company executives, and lawyers of all sorts.

Some astute observers have noted that in a representative democracy politicians will always have an image problem.[1] Their hold on public trust is unavoidably tenuous. It is not that their self-interested behavior is inherently offensive. The entire economic order, after all, is based on the premise that people act in self-interested ways. Politicians are distinctive, however, in that they represent themselves as acting in *our* interests—not their own. Often they do act in our interests, but they are self-interested as well, and this duplicity offends.

Furthermore, as Garry Wills has noted, politicians are always compromising their principles. They habitually seem to be "selling out." That is not the American Way, or at least it is not supposed to be. We admire those who stand on their principles and refuse to compromise. Paradoxically, politicians in a representative democracy must compromise in order to sustain the system. Each of us wants our own ideas to prevail in politics. A representative politician therefore must broker these competing claims in ways that will not be so offensive as to prevent election. Some compromise is inevitably a part of this process. Most nonpoliticians spend little time thinking about the differences between private and public life. To them, such compromising simply indicates a character flaw and increases their cynicism toward politicians and politics.

Political scientists tend to think about politics in a less tactical way. Strategies and tactics are of interest, but these are rarely regarded as *defining*, or even distinctive of, the world of politics. Typically, the point of departure for political scientists is the substantive result of strategies and tactics, and so politics is seen as integral to distribution. Definitions of politics are always contentious. None is completely satisfying. One that is broadly shared by political scientists, however, is that *politics is the authoritative allocation of values for society*.[2] Normally this process of allocation is observed in the context of governmental or quasi-governmental institutions. While this definition is not perfect, it does help to elucidate the concept of politics in a number of ways.

What does it mean to allocate, or distribute, values? Values are things desired and may be usefully conceived as being of two sorts. First, there are nonmaterial values which the political process often distributes or restricts. Does a woman have an inherent right to abort an at least potential child? What are appropriate limits of television violence? Can a local government display a nativity scene during the holiday season? Should the Confederate flag fly over the state capitol of South Carolina? Can pornographers use the Internet? While it might be argued that some of these questions contain a material component (pornographers can make money through the Internet, for example, and some doctors may benefit materially from legalized abortion) they are mostly nonmaterial. They raise the question, "What values should we value?" Even a casual observer will recognize that the political system is continuously involved with struggles to resolve such issues.

Values may also be material, that is, they may be tangible things that are desired. Here, too, the work of the political process is obvious. Who should be taxed, and how much? How much money should be spent on national defense, and who will get the resulting contracts? Where should roads be built? Should growing wheat be subsidized? Who is entitled to receive disability checks? Should there be import quotas on Japanese-built VCRs? Who is entitled to student financial aid? Such familiar questions underscore this core dimension of politics.

Politics is not the only process that distributes material goods in society. Another very powerful mechanism for doing so is the market, which is commonly considered to be "free," or wholly distinct from the realm of politics. In this society, people may buy peaches or pineapples, CDs featuring Gloria Estefan or Blink-182, food processors or frozen dinners, all according to their wherewithal and personal values. Unlike in some centrally controlled "command economies," the government does not intrude on such decisions.

However, to regard these decisions as either private or free is a misconception, for politics is inevitably involved in establishing the structure and boundaries of the market system. Despite the prevalence of contrary rhetoric, Americans recognize the need to control the market, and politics is the system that does. It establishes the rules of the game for the market economy. Americans do not believe, for example, that people should be bought and sold in the marketplace; nor should plutonium. They want to know that the meat they buy is not tainted, and that toys will not harm their children. They want automobiles to be manufactured in such a way as to not ravage the environment. They believe workers are entitled to safe working conditions, and that major corporations may be rescued from bad business decisions they have made. In these and in many other ways politics intrudes on the market's system of distributing goods.

The allocation of values involves struggle, and so there are always winners and losers in politics. A common American bromide holds that people should be free to do anything they wish, so long as they do not harm anyone else. The problem with this is that politics is almost exclusively about matters (values) in which people *do* feel they have something to gain or lose. Some people suffer from defense cuts; others gain. This holds for nonmaterial values as well, where gains and losses are less tangible. A proponent of prayer in public schools might well believe that no one is hurt by allowing this practice, but an opponent could easily disagree.

The *"authoritative* allocation of values" means that the allocative decisions are broadly accepted by citizens as legitimate. This does not mean that the decisions are universally liked, or that once decisions are made there can be no effort to overturn them. Liberals and conservatives may disagree with each other about a new welfare law, but they at least tentatively comply with the law even as some may seek to overturn it. There are exceptions to this general rule. Some who feel passionately about an issue, such as civil rights activists in the sixties and some abortion opponents today, may break the law and accept the punishment of the state. These acts of conscience, they hope, will goad other citizens and ultimately politicians into changing the law.

Allocating decisions "for society" is perhaps the most troublesome part of this definition of politics. Politics often involves decisions which are quite narrow and focused. Additionally, some very powerful private organizations like Microsoft make allocative decisions for society. Boundary questions, troublesome for any definition, are notorious for this part of the definition of politics. The term "for society" is meant to distinguish politics from what occurs in relatively cohesive groups, where values are also allocated, but only for members of that group. When a religious organization asks its members to fast during Ramadan, it is allocating values for the members of that group and is therefore not political. Should this group seek to have a law passed requiring fasting for the general public, it would become political.

The second term that needs to be considered is "democracy," an idea that has come into vogue comparatively recently. The term has been around for centuries, but for most of the history of western political thought it has represented an arrangement to be avoided. Americans think of themselves as a great democratic people, yet as late as the constitutional period the term "democrat" was widely considered to be an epithet. For the Founders' generation, a democrat was usually thought to be an unscrupulous scoundrel who pandered to the ill-conceived whims of the masses.

The American Revolution unleashed a surge of democratic sentiment that dismayed many of the Founders.[3] As that sentiment deepened in the nineteenth century, it proved irresistible, and now other principles of political organization seem arcane. While some may grouse about how ill-prepared people are to participate in political life, no one seriously proposes an alternative in which some segment of the society—the rich, the college educated, certified political scientists (some of whom are certifiable)—should govern. The collapse of the authoritarian regimes in eastern Europe and the emergence of fledgling democracies in other parts of the world have convinced many that the threshold of a world-wide democratic era is at hand. As never before, democracy seems to be an idea whose time has arrived.

Ironically the idea of democracy, to which Americans seem deeply committed, is not one that is clearly grasped. "Democracy" is a term frequently used in public discourse, and yet most Americans stumble when asked to define the term. Usually they will identify some feature of the political system with democracy, as if to suggest that because democracy is a term commonly used in political rhetoric, democracy must be, in some sense, what Americans do. A typical conversation about democracy in America might well begin with some statement to the effect that the term means "the people rule." When asked what it means for the people to rule, a common assertion is that in America people rule because we have elections. If it is noted that many authoritarian political systems also hold elections, the determined American democrat will usually fall back to the position that elections must provide "choices." But not just any choices will do. The choices must be meaningful to citizens, and in any case elections can only be a first step toward democratic governance, not its guarantor.

The true test of democracy is not how leaders are selected, but how political decisions are made. *A democratic government is one in which citizenship is broadly conferred in the adult community, and in which citizens have an approximately equal chance to influence the outcomes and policies of the government.*[4] It is a system in which no one is guaranteed to win and all are taken seriously. Obviously there is a utopian strain in this concept. The world is unlikely to have a society that is the perfect expression of this standard, but because the standard has content it does help sort out those societies which are more or less democratic, and it also helps answer whether some political change would move a system closer to, or pull it further from, a democratic ideal.

Americans seem comfortable with the idea of representative democracy. There are some occasions, such as state and local ballot initiatives, when citizens participate directly in policy formulation. For the most part, however, their participation in policy formulation occurs indirectly, through elected representatives. Therefore the democratic standard must be applicable along two dimensions: Citizens must have an approximately equal chance to influence both the selection of representatives as well as their subsequent political decisions.

Space has been given to the definitions of politics and democracy because these terms recur throughout this book and the reader must have a sense for how they are being used. We may now turn our attention directly to several American political curiosities: political participation, foreign aid, social welfare, income inequality, and crime and punishment.

POLITICAL PARTICIPATION

The notion that a democratic political system is the best form of governance is so broadly shared in U.S. society that it needs no public defense. World War II was fought to "make the world safe for democracy." Many Americans saw teleological significance in the collapse of the communist systems of eastern Europe, viewing it as the triumph of morality in a world fraught with evil. In the eyes of many, this country, as the modern world's first and still purest democratic nation, represents the crest of a mighty democratic wave splashing toward its total and inevitable triumph.

For all of the rhetorical commitment to democracy, however, Americans are less than exemplary practitioners of this form of governance. Most don't think very much about politics. A presidential address televised in prime time provokes more ire than interest, and enlarges the audience for reruns on local stations. At work or school, most people try to avoid political conversations. Levels of political knowledge and information are embarrassingly low. According to one systematic assessment of political knowledge,[5] majorities of American adults cannot name their U.S. representatives and senators. Nor do they know what common political terms like "conservative" and "liberal" mean. Substantive knowledge of policies being considered by the government is held by only a small fraction of the electorate, and still less is known about international affairs.

When thoughts turn to government, as has been noted, the typical American's estimation of it is very low. There has always been an antipolitical strain in America,[6] but in the early 1960s most adults expressed a great deal of trust and confidence in the Federal government, according to polls. The politically troubled sixties and especially Watergate undermined that faith, and the emergence of personality-driven television politics continued to nurture cynicism.[7]

Today people remain largely skeptical of government. Cynicism abounds, exemplified by popular movies such as *Dave* and *Wag the Dog*, and in the popularity of the nihilist humor that typifies late night talk shows. In a 1997 Gallup survey, less than one fifth of the population placed a great deal of faith in any of the national political institutions. Faith in politicians was the lowest ever recorded, as only 5 percent of the respondents said they placed a great deal of faith in people in public life. In 2000, a national survey reported 71 percent of Americans agreed with the statement, "Politics in America is generally pretty disgusting."[8]

Politicians sense this antipathy toward politics. In recent decades national political life has been replete with presidential candidates running against the rascals in Washington, and even against the idea of government itself. George Wallace, George McGovern, Jimmy Carter, Ronald Reagan, Jerry Brown, H. Ross Perot, Pat Buchanan, Jesse Ventura, and Bill Clinton variously used antigovernment themes to help propel themselves to national political prominence. President Reagan never let go of the idea that "government isn't the solution: it's the problem," even while serving for eight years in this nation's highest office. President Clinton prominently played on this theme as well, promising to "reinvent government."

The expression of this sentiment in political life reached a high water mark of sorts during 1995 when a Republican Congress and a Democratic president could not agree about balancing the budget. Congress refused to pass temporary measures to keep the government fiscally solvent as negotiations proceeded, and so for a few days the government closed "nonessential" operations. During this crisis Senator Phil Gramm, who was seeking the Republican presidential nomination, rhetorically asked a New Hampshire audience, "Does anyone miss the government?" Evidently people actually did. Public sentiment quickly forced the Republicans to backtrack. The government was reopened and Gramm's political campaign evaporated. It is interesting, however, that leaders of the majority party in Congress felt antigovernment sentiment was so deep that closing it down would be a good political tactic.

Political parties, as intermediate institutions connecting ordinary people to the process of government, once drew people into politics. That connection has become enfeebled. Increasingly, people feel that partisan attachment taints one with the stigma of politics. Between 1952 and 1996 the percentage of Americans not identifying with a major political party increased by half, to 34 percent of the electorate. Forty percent of the people between the ages of 18 and 29 considered themselves "independents" in 1996.[9] Citizens who energize a political system through sustained commitment are being replaced by consumers who are unattached to a party and select political leaders as if they were considering varieties of cheese.

Voting in elections has been on a downward slide since 1960, when 63 percent of the eligible electorate voted. In 1996 only 49 percent of the eligible electorate cast their votes in the presidential election, a rate far below that of the other established democracies. Turnout is 10 to 15 percent lower in off-year elections. One study of political participation[10] notes that with regard to other kinds of political activity—such as political campaigning, being active in a local community, or contacting government officials—Americans are as active as democratic citizens elsewhere. What is distinctive about American political participation, including voting, is that it is very unequally distributed across social class. Working class and less educated citizens participate far less than wealthier, better educated citizens, and also far less than their counterparts in the European democracies.

All of this creates a strange brew, and one that is distinctively American. The widespread belief in democracy is paralleled by the popular conviction that the United States is the appropriate exemplar of this form of government. Yet democracy requires broadly active, knowledgeable, attentive citizens if it is to flourish. Americans are far from that. Typically they are woefully ignorant about political affairs, not particularly active, unattached to, and cynical about, political life. What is particularly curious is the *simultaneous* holding of these views. The popular reverence for American democracy coupled with the aversion to politics is fraught with irony and brings to mind a comment from the comic strip Pogo, "We have seen the enemy and he are us."

FOREIGN AID

Most Americans have the perception that the United States is extremely generous with economic assistance to other nations. During the era of huge national budget deficits in the eighties and early nineties, many citizens felt that cutting back on economic assistance to developing nations was a good way to bring the deficit under control. This belief was based on wildly exaggerated notions of how much economic assistance this nation provided the rest of the world. In 1995 the Center for the Study of Policy Attitudes[11] asked a national sample of Americans whether they thought the government was spending too much, too little, or about the right amount of money on foreign aid. About three fourths of the respondents stated that too much money was being spent. A subsequent question asked for an estimation of the percentage of the U.S. budget that was going to foreign aid. The median estimate was 15 percent—fifteen times the actual number of 1 percent.

In the years following World War II, the United States did provide substantial economic assistance to other nations. The devastation caused by that war was such that America was one of the few industrialized nations with the capacity to provide assistance, a behemoth among the world's flattened or nondeveloped economies. In recent years, however, this contribution has declined significantly. Although the United States is still by far the wealthiest nation in the world, it ranked third in the world in development assistance in 1997 according to figures compiled by the Organization for Economic Cooperation and Development.[12] Both France and Japan contributed more than the United States. These contributions were measured in absolute terms. When assistance was figured as a percentage of gross national product—probably a fairer way to compute contributions—the United States fell to twenty-first, trailing such nations as Finland, Ireland, and Portugal.

Both the widespread belief in American generosity and the actual comparative stinginess of U.S. development assistance are individually interesting. The juxtaposition of the two is what makes them curious. The reality of U.S. stinginess is perhaps obscured by the broadly shared conviction that this nation is the world's Good Samaritan. Or perhaps this belief lingers as a residue from the post–war era, when contributions were more generous. But earlier foreign aid was not primarily based upon the idea that it had intrinsic worth. Far more compelling was the argument that foreign aid was prudent.[13] Overwhelmingly, foreign aid was justified by policy-makers as something that would help the United States win the Cold War with the Soviet Union. As the Cold War ebbed, so did U.S. giving.

SOCIAL WELFARE

David Lumsdaine's comprehensive study of international foreign assistance found that countries offering little foreign assistance tended also to have low levels of domestic social welfare expenditures. "Public concerns about poverty, expressed in domestic social spending and donations to international charitable causes, give strong, and increasingly strong, explanations of differences of aid spending between donors."[14] The United States is an example of the pattern Lumsdaine uncovered, where small foreign aid contributions are complemented by a modest commitment to social welfare spending. The United States is, for example, the only industrialized nation in the world without a comprehensive national health care program. As a result, the census bureau reported that in 1999 more than 44 million Americans, 16.3 percent of the population, have no health insurance. And that number is growing.[15] These are not the poorest citizens, who at least may qualify for government-sponsored Medicaid. Typically, the uninsured do work, but their jobs either do not provide medical benefits or have packages in which the worker share of the premium is out of reach.

The weakness of the national commitment to helping the poorest members of its society is another distinctive feature of American politics. Most Americans do believe in helping the "truly needy." During the early days of President Reagan's administration, government assistance to the poor was cut substantially, yet even during this time there was public rhetoric about maintaining a "safety net" to help the "truly needy." Americans just happen to believe that not many of this sort exist.

Although they may believe in helping the truly needy, Americans tend to be suspicious of those on welfare. Instead of seeing poor people as the victims of social forces mostly beyond their control, Americans are more likely to think of them as being morally deficient or lazy. Popular consciousness teems with stories of welfare queens driving Cadillacs, of women having babies to increase the amount of their welfare checks, and of irresponsible purchases with food stamps. It matters not that careful analysis of welfare recipients and assistance programs contradicts these popular images. The will to cling to these misconceptions remains undaunted.

Americans also believe that their government spends much more on welfare than it actually does. During the 1995 national debates on welfare reform, a New York *Times*/CBS poll asked Americans to estimate the percentage of the federal budget that was spent on welfare.[16] On average, respondents estimated that about 25 percent of the federal budget went to social welfare. This question came amid a series of questions about welfare mothers and children, and so it is quite likely that most respondents were thinking of programs like Aid For Families with Dependent Children in answering this question. AFDC was .1 percent of the federal budget in 1994. Even if it is assumed that the respondents were thinking of all kinds of social welfare—including cash benefits for disabled people, pregnant women's nutrition programs, aid to needy veterans, school lunch and breakfast programs, nutrition programs for the elderly, all housing programs and so forth—total budget allocations rise to only 8.5 percent, far below average estimates of the respondents.

During the administration of Richard Nixon, presidential advisor Milton Friedman proposed a minimum guaranteed income for all Americans. As a conservative libertarian economist, Dr. Friedman was no friend of government. He defended his proposal on the grounds of efficiency. In his view, a simple check-writing plan was far more efficient and less costly than a variety of specific welfare programs. Despite his prestige, Dr. Friedman's proposal went nowhere. He underestimated the moral point of the welfare system. Because Americans are suspicious of people on welfare, they prefer programs that keep an eye on them.

Occasionally the inadequacies of poor people are cast in terms of an absence of relevant skills, and consequently there have been policy gestures toward job training. This perspective resonates weakly with cultural values and so such programs are more often the subjects of criticism and inadequate financing. The more powerful belief about the character of poor people points policy in the direction of invasive welfare programs. Americans prefer that poor people be watched, poked, and prodded. to be assured that they are looking for work, to have welfare agents visit their homes to check for possible irregularities, and to have them make frequent and demeaning trips to the welfare office. Americans want poor people, in the words of welfare analyst George Gilder, to feel "the spur of their poverty."[17] This statement outraged liberal critics of Gilder, but there is not any evidence to suggest that the average American was upset by it. The virtue of food stamps, for example, is that they impose on their bearers an easily observed stigma, the scarlet letter of contemporary social life. They place welfare recipients on public display, giving others a chance to observe their spending habits.

Recent economic trends shed additional light on the way Americans tend to think about poor people. The sluggishness of the national economy during the 1970s proved to be a political albatross for both Presidents Ford and Carter. It was an important factor in voters' rejection of each of these presidents as they sought reelection. The economic malaise of the seventies grew to a crisis during the first two years of the Reagan administration, as the ranks of the unemployed swelled to double digits for the first time since the Great Depression. At about the midpoint of President Reagan's first term, however, the economy began to improve. Growth returned, slowing for a time during the Bush administration, and then taking off dramatically during the Clinton term.

There was something interesting about the 1982–95 recovery, however. In contrast to the long period of growth that occurred after World War II, the fruits of this latter growth spurt were not broadly shared. In the earlier period, the rich got richer, but the fortunes of others improved as well, with the result that the number of people living in poverty declined substantially. The fruits of the later recovery were not shared in this way. The rich grew richer, but the percentage of people living in poverty *increased* during this time. A careful examination of these two periods by policy analysts indicates that the major reason poverty grew during the second period was because of structural changes in the economy, especially in labor markets. Unlike the post–war period, the recovery did not produce enough jobs of the sort that would pull people out of poverty.[18]

Academic analysis notwithstanding, Americans tended to blame increasing poverty on poor people themselves and on the programs designed to assist them. Such feelings were undoubtedly stimulated by the national debate on welfare reform in 1995, as Republican and Democratic leaders alike characterized the welfare system as a disaster *because* of the growth of poverty. It was like saying that fire fighters are failures because they do not prevent fires. As politicians are usually prudent, it is culturally interesting that alternative explanations of poverty carried so little resonance. Perhaps in part due to the rhetoric of the time, the New York *Times*/CBS poll cited earlier reported that 96 percent of the respondents indicated that the welfare system needed to be fundamentally changed.

And so Democratic President Clinton and a Republican Congress collaborated on a plan of "welfare reform." These reforms ended the policy, established during the New Deal, that welfare was an entitlement, that is, something to which one is entitled so long as qualifications are met. The total federal dollar commitment to welfare was reduced, and that money distributed to individual states to allow them to devise their own programs. Time limits for welfare assistance were established, but there were no concomitant requirements for job training, job placement, or child care. In short, welfare was reformed by cutting it and pushing people off it.[19] This bipartisan effort, more than anything else, is a solid indication of American attitudes toward welfare. The severity of the effects of this policy shift has been attenuated by continued rapid economic growth. The true test for it will come with the next economic downturn.

INCOME INEQUALITY

A related political curiosity concerns patterns of income inequality existing in society. Any pattern of income distribution is dependent upon the social norms and political rules of that society. In human history, a huge array of such patterns have existed. In some societies, for example, the material wealth generated has gone to a ruling family because that is what the norms dictated. The privileges and leisure of the ruling family were accepted as part of the right order of things.

It is easy for Americans to see that the leaders of such societies have "pulled a fast one" on their people. It is less obvious that patterns of wealth distribution in modern industrial societies are socially and politically determined as well. Politics may be the authoritative allocation of values, but the implication of this escapes most citizens. Most feel that the system of accumulation existing in the United States is not due to social convention but is instead part of the larger order of things. Rather than a social construct, the pattern seems to accord with the laws of nature. Those with "the right stuff" make it; those without it fail. In the 1996 Presidential campaign, Robert Dole proposed a substantial across-the-board tax cut. He justified his proposal in terms familiar to the conventional wisdom: "It's your money. You earned it. You should be allowed to keep it."

Mr. Dole's refrain undercut the conventional wisdom, however, even as it sought to extend it. Implicit in his slogan is the recognition that patterns of distribution are determined by social rules. Americans could decide, for example, not to use public funds to build highways and instead let people fend for themselves, making roads wherever they wanted or could. Or education could be conceived as a private matter not needing public investment. Such decisions would reduce the need for federal income and allow people to keep more of "their" money. On the other hand, Americans might decide that the social prestige that comes with being CEO of a corporation is in itself substantial reward, and therefore that no CEO could earn more than four times the salary of the corporation's lowest paid employee. Obviously, the new patterns of allocation resulting from these decisions would not accord with any law of nature. They would simply result from alternative social conventions.

Beginning in the early years of the Reagan administration, tax laws were changed that, in combination with cuts in social programs, redistributed wealth upward along the social scale. The rich got richer, the poor, poorer. In the Clinton administration a tax increase on wealthier citizens marginally slowed the growth of inequality. Still, because of decisions made by government officials, the tax system is more regressive today than it was in the 1950s. Middle- and working-class Americans are paying proportionately more than they once did. Patterns of inequality are directly connected to such decisions.

An important reason for increased economic inequality is the shift from an industrial to a service economy. One consequence of this is that well-paying jobs in the industrial sector are disappearing and are being replaced by not-so-well-paying jobs in the service sector. Steel workers are being replaced by fast food employees. In contrast to changes in tax laws, one tends to think that the government has little to do with these ineluctable economic trends. Economic restructuring is regarded as "natural." This is not the case. Through tariffs, spending initiatives, varying rules about relocation, and so forth, governments nurture some industries and undermine others. One of the reasons labor unions so adamantly opposed the NAFTA free trade agreement with Canada and Mexico was because they believed it would reduce well-paying jobs in this country.

The point of these examples is not to demonstrate that one set of decisions is better than another. How much the wealthy *ought* to pay in taxes, what kinds of things taxes should pay for, whether NAFTA is good or bad for the country, are matters to be resolved by the political process. Such examples are raised to illustrate that patterns of social wealth are not inherently right; they are matters of social convention. James Fallows[20] indicates how different assumptions can dramatically alter social policies by contrasting the economic theories of Adam Smith, whose thought has dramatically influenced American economists, with that of Friedrich List, little known in the United States but very important to German and Japanese economists. One difference is sufficient to illustrate the point. The primary concern of Smith is how individuals fare as consumers. Take care of individuals and the larger society will automatically take care of itself. In contrast, List argues that real world happiness depends on more than how much money individuals take home. If people around you are also comfortable, you are happier and safer than if they are desperate. Therefore, List believed, some attention needs to be given to collective, as well as individual, well-being. Such contrasting assumptions will have a significant impact on the social rules of distribution.

The American distributive system has resulted in the most unequal pattern of rewards in the western, industrialized world. And economic inequality is growing. In 1996, the fourth year of a long economic recovery, census bureau data on income trends show that the top 5 percent of households received 21.4 percent of national income, the highest since the bureau began reporting such data in 1967. An analysis of Congressional Budget Office data from 1977 through 1999 reveals that the after tax income of the wealthiest 1 percent of the population shot up 115 percent. Incomes of the wealthiest fifth of the population grew by 43 percent during this period, the middle three fifths income growth was a little less than eight percent, and the poorest fifth of the population saw their proportion of income shrink by 9 percent. The distribution of wealth, which includes assets as well as income, is even more unequal. In 1950, the top 1 percent of the population owned 28 percent of the wealth; in 1996, they owned 38 percent. Such trends are distinctively American. The richest 20 percent of Americans is *thirteen* times richer than the poorest 20 percent. In France, the factor is six and in Japan it is four.[21]

Fully as interesting as the extent of economic inequality is the fact that this pattern is not a topic of public discussion. Given the fundamental concerns of politics, one might expect it to be subject to sustained public scrutiny, but this is not the case. Economic inequality is virtually ignored in presidential election campaigns. To the extent that it is raised at all, it is raised by those whose policies would result in even greater inequality— the flat taxers. It was the centerpiece of Steve Forbes's presidential bids, for example. In an early kickoff to his 2000 campaign, he spoke in favor of the flat tax, saying, "We need to take the current tax code and kill it, drive a stake through its heart, bury it, and hope it never rises again to terrorize the American people."[22] The image of multimillionaire Forbes living in terror of the tax system is arresting.

CRIME AND PUNISHMENT

Whether formally or informally, all societies codify standards of behavior for their members, and specify the consequences for violating these norms. Because politics is the authoritative allocation of values for society, it is integrally concerned with these prescriptions. Several things are culturally interesting about crime and punishment in the United States.

One of these is the army of professionals whose purpose is determining the boundaries of these norms. Because national legal systems vary dramatically, comparative data are problematic, but a University of Wisconsin study estimates that the United States has between 25 and 35 percent of the world's lawyers.[23] Why so many? One major reason is that the United States is a litigious society. Americans are quick to sue and to be sued. Rather than resolving differences informally, which requires a reasonable amount of trust, Americans show a marked tendency to use official legal machinery. Scholars have always considered U.S. litigation rates to be high, and one study noted a 24 percent increase in litigation between 1984 and 1990.[24] A citizen is far more likely to have direct contact with the courts than with any other part of the political system.

A large number of lawyers is also hired by corporations or by law firms servicing the corporate sector. Legal assistance is necessary for routine purposes—such as assuring the legitimacy of a contract—because corporations are likely to sue or be sued by other corporations and citizens, and to insure that operations are being conducted within legal constraints. Corporate executives commonly complain about the government's imposition of bureaucratic red tape. A favorite villain is the government bureaucrat who regularly requires the entrepreneur to fill out mountains of paperwork, thereby stifling initiative. Government regulation has grown more complex in some areas, and this complexity might sometimes be unnecessary. But complexity does not simply evolve in a vacuum. Most of the time it is responsive. One major reason complexity has increased is because of the phalanx of lawyers hired by business interests whose major purpose is helping those interests uphold the letter of the law while violating its spirit.[25] In such an environment, bureaucratic complexity is inevitable.

Perhaps the most familiar reason for the number of lawyers is the high level of crime, especially violent crime, in the United States. Criminal activity is an old American story and, as we shall see in the next chapter, criminals are not without their romantic pull on American consciousness.[26] In recent years, crime rates have diminished. Analysts commonly identify the aging of the huge baby boom cohort (old folks are less likely to commit crimes) and the broad economic expansion (in 1999 unemployment reached a thirty-year low) as important reasons for the decline in criminal activity. Such trends should not mask the comparative American inclination for crime.

It can at least be argued that the United States is not the most *violent* society in the world. One can think of places in eastern Europe, the Middle East, and Africa that are more violent. In such areas, however, the legitimacy of the society itself is in question. Conflict in Palestine or Bosnia, for example, grows out of the fact that people sharing a common space cannot agree on appropriate governing authority. Values allocation is not authoritative. In this sense they are not societies at all. The violence grows out of deep seated religious, ethnic, or regional conflict. Distressing as it is, this violence is at least comprehensible.

The United States has its share of racial, ethnic, and religious strife. Hate groups proliferate. Racial and ethnically based gangs engage in territorial struggles. The type of violence described in the previous paragraph is evident in the United States as well. However, this society is unique in its level of what may be called nihilistic violence—that is, violence that seems born out of nothing more than some inner sense of personal rage. Someone climbs to the top of a university clock tower and fires randomly on unknown students passing below. Someone else enters a drugstore and laces a bottle of Tylenol with a deadly poison. Another person drops concrete blocks off a freeway overpass. Still others enter fast food franchises, elementary schools, post offices, and other places, and randomly spray bullets on innocent victims. An eighty-year-old woman is raped and robbed of three dollars. Such crimes *are* distinctively American, and any explanation of our political culture must be able to account for them.

The *response* to lawbreaking is as interesting as the *level* of law breaking. Why people seem so unattached to the rules of the society, or how they may be bound more closely to the social order, are questions that are rarely asked. Instead, attention is overwhelmingly devoted to punishing law breakers. In contrast to popular notions of judicial leniency and coddling of criminals, U.S. courts send people to jail more frequently, and for longer periods of time, than almost any other country. A 1995 report on international rates of incarceration shows that the United States puts more of its citizens behind bars than any other nation of the world except Russia, a nation that is barely functional. Other nations closest to the United States in rates of incarceration are former states of the old Soviet Union. The western industrialized country closest to the United States on this list is New Zealand, which ranks twentieth. The U.S. rate of incarceration is four times greater than New Zealand's, and six times that of England, which ranks in the middle of the nations of the world.[27] And a Justice Department study showed that, from 1990 through 1998, the U.S. prison population grew at an average annual rate of 6.2 percent. Despite the falling crime rates, the proportion of the U.S. population behind bars is now the highest in our history. With just 5 percent of the world's population, the United States has a quarter of the world's prisoners.[28]

This extraordinary rate of incarceration reflects a national sentiment that supports getting tougher on criminals as a solution to crime. In recent decades it has been a major theme of Republican presidential campaigns. Democratic President Clinton, who had signaled his toughness on crime by ordering the execution of a mentally retarded Arkansas man during the 1992 campaign, stole some Republican thunder with his own crime prevention package. The centerpiece of his crime package was a promise to use federal funds to place more police officers on the street. To some fanfare, Governor George W. Bush interrupted his 2000 presidential primary struggle with John McCain, jetting to his home state of Texas to preside over the execution of a prisoner.

Thus, it is not surprising that prison populations are swelling. The popular support for the "three strikes and you're out" movement as a solution to crime is tangible evidence of the continuing interest in toughness. Passed by popular referendum in California, this movement has spread to other states as well. These laws vary from state to state, but the general intent is to remove sentencing discretion from judges in cases of second and third serious offenses. Those convicted in such circumstances are required to serve sentences two or three times the length prescribed by law.

Children have not been spared from this get tough policy. Increasingly juvenile offenders are being treated as adults in the judicial system. In recent years, twenty states have lowered the minimum age for the death penalty to 16, and four more have lowered it to 17. The juvenile crime bill passed by the House in 1999 would allow youth as young as thirteen to be tried as adults in the federal system, following the growing practice of state court systems.[29] The belief that juveniles are not fully accountable for their actions and that they therefore should be treated with greater leniency and with more intervention than are adults is in retreat. This new federal shift in emphasis, echoing trends in numerous states, means that children are regarded as fully accountable for their actions. Thirteen-year-olds convicted under this bill would be swept into the nation's adult correctional facilities. In Michigan recently, a thirteen-year-old boy was tried as an adult and convicted of second degree murder for an act he committed when he was 11. In their 2000 primary, California voters passed Proposition 21 by a margin of 62–38 percent. This proposition sought to transfer the authority to decide whether to try juveniles as adults from judges to *prosecutors*.[30]

In this climate, it is not surprising that correctional costs have become a major government expense, representing one of the few significant growth areas in state budgets. In state after state, correctional costs claim a larger proportion of state revenues. After World War II and continuing into the 1970s, California established perhaps the world's most prestigious system of public higher education. Anchored by the University of California at Berkeley, and the rest of the university system, it included a substantial and well-funded state university system as well. But in recent years this system has fallen on hard times. It has been faced with increasing budgetary constraints, and student fees and tuition are rapidly increasing. In the meantime, correctional expenditures in California have skyrocketed. In 1995, for the first time in its history, the state spent more on prisons than on its two university systems.[31] California's story is repeated in state after state. Between 1987 and 1995, state general fund spending on higher education declined by an average of 18.2 percent, while spending on corrections rose 30 percent, according to the 1996 report of the National Association of State Budget Officers.[32]

Perhaps the greatest curiosity of the American justice system is the growing tendency to remand those who have been convicted of violations of public law to private, profit-seeking correctional institutions. Today, about 7 percent of the adult prison population is housed in such institutions, but private facilities are growing at four times the rate of government institutions. This stunning retreat from public responsibility has given rise to what one analyst has called a "prison-industrial complex." In this system the economic incentives encourage increasing the number of prisoners and the length of sentences. In contrast, there are disincentives for rehabilitation, because requisite programs and professionals cost money.[33] Theoretically, private prisons are subject to government guidelines, but there is already evidence of indifferent enforcement of these guidelines. A major investigative report by the Chicago *Tribune* on profit-seeking juvenile facilities, which house 40 percent of juvenile offenders, found significant corruption, including keeping children beyond their scheduled release dates, skimping on food, and ill-trained, minimum wage "correction officers." One New Orleans judge recently ordered the release of a 17-year-old from the private Jena Jail, owned and operated by the Wackenhut Corrections Corporation, because of abuse by guards. The judge, who visited the facility before issuing his verdict, found abuse to be widespread, despite the existence of formal regulations. He commented that the jail, "treats juveniles as if they walked on all fours."[34]

The American system of crime and punishment is an interesting commentary on the nature of social commitment. The high rate of crime, the propensity to sue, a unique capacity for nihilist crime, all suggest a casual attachment to the social order. And the social system responds in kind, with longer and more punitive sentences extending even to children, and with the growing trend of "for profit" prisons and the inevitable diminution of public responsibility. The lack of attachment, the absence of a sense of shared lives, runs both ways.

SUMMARY

The patterns described in this chapter are not the only distinctive features of the political system, but collectively they characterize an interesting way of thinking about and doing politics. Anyone wishing to understand American politics must provide some sort of explanation for the outcomes that have been described. It is possible to treat each of these phenomena idiosyncratically, as if there were no connections among them. This approach is useful. Each pattern is, after all, complex and doubtless to some degree distinctive. Prime time television and local news programming, for example, are more central to understanding American attitudes about crime than they are to understanding attitudes about foreign aid.

A second way to understand the five patterns is to look for things that bind them, to consider whether they are part of a larger pattern that also illuminates how the political system works. This approach is also useful. One common explanation of this sort ties various political outcomes to more fundamental economic forces. Scratch the surface of any given political pattern, this view holds, and one will find the forces of raw economic power at work.

The approach of this book is to consider such patterns through the prism of political culture. This approach neither gainsays the importance of the other two perspectives, nor asserts the primacy of a cultural perspective. The forces shaping particular political outcomes are, at some level, unique. And there can be little doubt that economic factors are crucial to political life in this or any other country. There is no shortage of these sorts of explanations, however. Case studies abound, as do economic explanations of the state.

The contention here is that the understanding of American politics can be enhanced by considering important aspects of the political culture. The curiosities described in this chapter are not *merely* random occurrences. They are connected. And for all the power it exerts in political life, capitalism in America is quite different from capitalism in Sweden or China. Political outcomes are not completely explained by autonomous economic forces. For these reasons then, political culture, far less frequently considered in explaining political outcomes, is important. And it is to some of the more important characteristics of American political culture that we now turn.

NOTES

1. See, for example, Michael Walzer, "Political Action: The Problem of Dirty Hands," *Philosophy and Public Affairs*, Vol. 2, No. 2, 1973, p. 160, and Garry Wills, "Hurrah for Politicians," *Harper's*, September, 1975, pp. 45–50.
2. David Easton first offered this definition of politics, and it remains as good as any. See Ch. V of his work, *The Political System*, New York: Alfred A. Knopf, 1966.
3. See Gordon S. Wood, *The Radicalism of the American Revolution*, New York: Vintage, 1993, esp. Ch. 19.
4. For an excellent and concise discussion of the concept of democracy, see Robert A. Dahl, *On Democracy*, New Haven, CT: Yale University Press, 1998.
5. Michael X Delli Carpini and Scott Keeter, *What Americans Know and Why It Matters*, Ch. 2. New Haven, CT: Yale University Press, 1996.
6. For an evocative history of antigovernment sentiment, see Garry Wills, *A Necessary Evil: A History of American Distrust of Government*, New York: Simon and Schuster, 2000.
7. See W. Lance Bennett, *The Governing Crisis*, New York: St Martin's, 1996, and James Fallows, *Breaking The News*, New York: Vintage, 1997, for excellent accounts of the role of TV news in nurturing popular disconnection and cynicism.
8. *The Gallup Poll,* "Americans' Faith Shaken But Not Shattered By Watergate," November 11,1997, www.gallup.com/poll/news/970619.htm. The "disgusting" data are from a poll taken by the Joan Shorenstein Center for the Press, Politics, and Public Policy at Harvard University, as part of the Vanishing Voter Project, March 13, 2000. www.vanishingvoter.org/releases/03-13-00.shtml.
9. Harold W. Stanley and Richard G. Giemi, *Vital Statistics on American Politics,* Washington, DC: Congressional Quarterly Inc., 1998, pp. 108–111.
10. Sidney Verba, Kay Lehman Schlozman, Henry E. Brady, *Voice and Equality: Civic Voluntarism and American Politics*, Cambridge, MA: Harvard University Press, 1995.
11. These results were taken from a poll conducted jointly by the Center for the Study of Policy Attitudes and the Center for International and Securities

Studies, University of Maryland: "Americans and Foreign Aid, January 23, 1995." www.info.usaid.gov/welcome/polls.

12. OECD figures are taken from "America the Stingy," Walter B. Gibbs, Minneapolis *Star Tribune*, p. A18, November 12, 1998.

13. David Halloran Lumsdaine, *Moral Vision in International Politics*, Princeton, NJ: Princeton University Press, 1993.

14. Lumsdaine, *op.cit.*, p.125.

15. Robert Pear, "44.3 million uninsured for health benefits," *The Chicago Tribune*, October 4, 1999, Sec. 1, p.3.

16. *New York Times*/CBS Poll, April 4, 1995. American Public Opinion Data (microfilm).

17. George Gilder, *Wealth and Poverty*, New York: Basic Books, 1981, p. 117.

18. Stanley Danzinger and Peter Gottschalk, *America Unequal*, Boston, MA: Harvard University Press, 1995, Ch.5.

19. See Mary Jo Bane, "Welfare As We Might Know It," *The American Prospect*, January–February, 1997, and Peter Edelman, "The Worst Thing Bill Clinton Has Done," *The Atlantic Monthly*, March, 1997.

20. James Fallows, "How the World Works," *The Atlantic Monthly*, December 1995.

21. R.C. Longworth, "A Bottom Line Blight on American Life," *The Chicago Tribune*, October 5, 1997, Section 2, p.1. The analysis of CBO 1977–1999 data was conducted by the Center on Budget and Policy Priorities.

22. Steve Forbes, An address to the Conservative Leadership Conference, Washington DC, November 23, 1996.

23. "Are There Too Many Lawyers?" New York State Bar Association, www.nysba.org/media/faq/toomany.html.

24. Lawrence Baum, *American Courts*, Third Edition, 1994, New York: Houghton Mifflin, p. 246.

25. See William Greider, *Who Will Tell The People*, New York: Touchstone, 1993, especially Ch. 4.

26. For a good history of crime in America, see Charles E. Silberman, *Criminal Violence, Criminal Justice*, New York: Random House, 1978. For a provocative reflection on the romance of crime, see Richard Slotkin, *Gunfighter Nation*, New York: Harper Perennial, 1993.

27. "Americans Behind Bars: U.S. and International Use of Incarceration 1995" www.sproject.com/press-11.htm.

28. Associated Press story, "Doubling of prison population has U.S. on track to be the leading jailer," *The Chicago Tribune*, March 15, 1999, Section 1, p.15.

29. The Sentencing Project Briefing Paper: "Prosecuting Juveniles in Adult Court." www.sproject.com/test/brief/juveniles.html

30. "Boy, 13, convicted of second-degree murder," Associated Press story carried in *The Chicago Tribune*, November 17, 1999. Section 1, p. 19.

31. Fox Butterfield, "New Prisons Cast Shadow Over Higher Education," *New York Times*, April 12, 1995, Section I, p. 9.

32. "1995 State Expenditure Report," April 1996 National Association of State Budget Officers, www.nasbo.org/pub/exprpt.exrp95es.htm.

33. Steven R. Donziger, "Fear, Crime, and Punishment in the United States," *Tikkun*, Vol. 12, No.6, pp. 24–27.

34. David Jackson and Cornelia Grumman, *Chicago Tribune* Investigative Report, "How Troubled Youth Became Big Business," September 26, 27, 28, 1999; "The Punishing Decade: Prison and Jail Estimates at the Millennium," Justice Policy Institute Report, Jason Zeidenberg and Vincent Schiraldi; the Jena Jail story was carried on the March 16, 2000, "All Things Considered" National Public Radio news program, www.npr.org.

3

Making It Alone

In any society, people inevitably approach politics with attitudes and dispositions that structure the way they think. In the United States, one of the building blocks of these attitudes, a principle construct of the political culture, is individualism. Personal experience is too rich for a single value to be universally shared, but individualism probably cuts as deeply in this society as any. As a cultural value it is, in a sense, prepolitical. Americans are schooled in individualism long before they begin to think seriously about politics, but this way of framing the world has a dramatic impact on political life.

As it is used here, individualism is the abiding conviction that people are personally responsible for their fates. Achievement in the world is largely a matter of individual choices. We are reluctant to recognize social structures that impede, enhance, or otherwise affect the character of our lives, and notions of interconnection and shared fates are downplayed. "Life" to Americans is the story of people making their way in the world in the presence of other more or less solitary souls doing the same thing. Occasionally, of course, one may have extraordinary good or bad luck, but individualism holds that people mostly get what they deserve in this world. In the manner of Horatio Alger novels, obstacles tend to be reconfigured as challenges providing the opportunity to demonstrate merit. This perspective has an ethical dimension as well. That is, Americans tend to believe both that individualism describes the way the world actually works, as well as that it is good for the world to work this way.

Americans share an idealized collective image of the good life known as the American Dream. The fact that the dream is so commonly referenced in everyday life is interesting in itself. One never hears of the French Dream or the Peruvian Dream, for example. Nevertheless, the human experience has generated numerous utopian ideas that seem to be of a kindred spirit with the American Dream. This is true only in the sense that the dreams share the quality of reflection about an ideal life. The American Dream is in fact quite distinctive, and this distinctiveness highlights an even more interesting quality. Unlike other utopian images, it is not animated by some vision of a magnificent city-state in which happiness is a function of the quality of a shared social life. Rather, the American Dream has been deeply influenced by individualist values. It is intensely private and thoroughly egocentric, a dream of individual struggle toward a life of personal ease, control, security, and comfort. The American Dream is largely indifferent to the plight of one's neighbors, one's community, even to the nation itself. It is in fact a collection of millions of private dreams that seemingly bear no relationship to each other.

Individualism flows out of the 18th century enlightenment and it therefore resonates in many and diverse cultures. Its effects on American life are unique, however, and this uniqueness is evident in the unusual reverence in which it is held. Perhaps more than any other idea, individualism serves as a constitutive myth for our society. It is a cornerstone of our culture. All societies must, in one way or another, balance the apparently contrasting drives for individualism and community. Kenneth Burke's definition of human beings, discussed in Chapter One, suggests that the need for both is inherent in the human species. In seeking a balance between these two needs, no other culture has tilted more sharply in the direction of individualism.

The importance of personal space deserves to be underscored. People need some room to be themselves, to exercise what is normally called liberty. Popular futuristic novels, such as *Brave New World* and *1984*, not to mention movies like *Blade Runner* and *Star Wars*, address deeply held fears of a time when the sphere of personal autonomy has evaporated and lives are dominated by a corporate/state apparatus. Evidence of the quality of life in actual totalitarian societies is even more compelling. American fears of repressive tyranny are as old as the Republic itself. George Washington had to contend with Shay's Rebellion, and U.S. history is replete with examples of individuals and groups who believe the larger community has suppressed crucial liberties, and who have therefore taken the law into their own hands. The roots of this impulse are at least in part psychological. Even in total institutions, such as prisons or mental hospitals, studies show that people go to extraordinary lengths to maintain personal identity.[1]

People need more than personal space, however. They also need a sense of order which comes out of the recognition of shared fates. Some kind of life in common is also part of human destiny, which is an important reason why cultures are necessary. Hence, the individualist strain of American culture is ironic: Americans *share* a constitutive myth that elides the idea of shared fates. Because individualism so undervalues common needs and the legitimacy of interdependence, the purpose of social life is obscured. Individualism seems to imply that people come together in order to have nothing to do with each other. This is a strange sort of bonding, and one that is rife with tension. Patriotic leaders constantly refer to the United States as "the land of the free," and the inscription on the Statue of Liberty invites people here who yearn to "breathe free." Such freedom is what Isaiah Berlin has called "negative freedom,"[2] that is, freedom as absence of constraint. It is the sort of freedom that allows "doing your own thing" without bothering about, or being bothered by, others. Any society is *inherently* constraining, however. Some of these constraints are conscious, and knowingly accepted. Others are preconscious and are accepted instinctively. Purely negative freedom is problematic for social life. If it were truly a foundational human concern, one wonders why societies, with their necessary and inherent constraints, would ever be established.

Alexis De Tocqueville was the first in a series of eminent commentators to notice the individualist strain in U.S. culture. The idea of individualism was relatively new in intellectual circles when he visited America in 1831. Tocqueville was the first serious social theorist to use the term in a major work, and it is instructive that its use comes in reflections on America. This distinctive aspect of U.S. culture intrigued him greatly. For Tocqueville, individualism is "a calm and considered feeling which disposes each citizen to isolate himself from the mass of his fellows and withdraw into the circle of family and friends; with this little society formed to his taste, he gladly leaves the greater society to look after itself." The danger that Tocqueville saw in individualism was that it could easily evolve into egoism, which is "a passionate and exaggerated love of self which leads a man to think of all things in terms of himself and to prefer himself to all."[3]

Tocqueville worried that individualism could potentially subvert a democratic society, but he felt that its socially debilitative effects were countered through institutional structure in nineteenth-century America. Political institutions and voluntary associations served as useful antidotes to the potentially destructive excesses of individualism. We shall return to his thoughts on this matter toward the end of the chapter.

Why are Americans so uniquely attracted to this idea? One possibility, and there is certainly truth in this claim, is that individualism is inherently appealing. A powerful case can be made for individualist values such as personal choice, autonomy, unique development, and personal responsibility. But this kind of response does not answer the *cultural* question, for the values generated by individualism are not the only important social values, and the fact is that other cultures are less smitten with the ethos of individualism than are Americans.

Popular advocates of this cultural norm might respond, however, that rationality leads to an individualist ethic, and that citizens of other cultures are less individualist because they lack insight. If they could see more clearly, the appeals of individualism would become more apparent to them. As the most enlightened nation of the world, such advocates might argue, it is not surprising to find other cultures lagging in the American wake. The idea of the United States as world exemplar is a very old one. Many early European immigrants believed they were leaving behind a world that had seriously gone wrong. The "New World" had both literal and metaphorical significance. From the time of John Winthrop's ringing declaration in 1630 that the proper destiny of Pilgrim groups was to establish a shining "city on a hill" which would be an example for the rest of the world, there have been those who have supported this idea. President Reagan extended this long tradition by citing Winthrop's phrase in his second inaugural address.

The argument that the characteristics of the culture flow from purely rational choice is ultimately unconvincing, however. Cultures typically are ethnocentric and self-justifying. The Chinese, the British, the Japanese, the French, to name only an obvious few, tend to look at other societies as if they do not have things quite right. It is always tempting to believe that one's culture is the closest to eternal truth, the one that most clearly perceives the world. At present, this temptation may be particularly great. The adoption of market systems in eastern Europe and China naturally encourages the belief that the world is coming to accept the American Way. The market system may in fact push the Chinese, for example, toward a more individualistic culture, but partly because of cultural variation, markets work differently in different parts of the world. The Chinese and Eastern Europeans hope to improve on what the United States has done, to achieve a higher synthesis by merging the market system with their own traditions.

The fact that cultures tend to ratify structures of power that already exist in a society also suggests caution with respect to the rational choice hypothesis. Important political stakes are involved in the dissemination and internalization of core values. The powerful in any society will seek to maintain that power by promoting cultural patterns and institutions that will help them do so. Certainly the individualist ethos works in this way. If "making it" in the world is a matter of personal choice and effort, then those at the top of the social ladder deserve to be there, while those at the bottom deserve their fates as well. If everyone deserves his or her fate, then any appeals to upset the status quo are automatically suspect. In particular, individualism encourages the view that those at the bottom of the social and economic structure are victims, not of larger social forces, but of their own ineptitude. It is possible, in other words, that Americans have been duped into believing so ardently in individualism.

Thus, arguments concerning the intrinsic merit of any cultural characteristic such as individualism should be treated with some skepticism. Perhaps the characteristic does represent a right ordering of the world. Then again, perhaps not. Rather than suggest that cultural characteristics are good or bad, the task should be to see them clearly, to learn how they developed and are sustained, and to consider their political consequences. And since cultures tend to be self-ratifying, their problematic aspects need to be identified.

INDIVIDUALISM AND THE U.S. RELIGIOUS TRADITION

Focusing as it does on ultimate concern, religion is inevitably important in the formation of a culture. An exception might be a society that is not particularly religious, but not many of these exist, and it is certainly not true of the United States. Garry Wills has examined the U.S. religious tradition and demonstrated convincingly—contrary to what some have argued— a deep and enduring religious commitment.[4] The religious tradition in the United States is both rich and varied, and it is impossible to do it justice in a book of this sort. One part of that tradition, however, has been especially influential in cultural development and in the promotion of individualism—the Protestant tradition of the American colonials. The religious ideas of the people who emigrated from Europe during the colonial period played a huge role in the developing American culture. Those who held these views dominated the social structure and ultimately established an integrated political system. Not only were early cultural patterns established by them, but religious sentiment was especially important to them. Although their religious ideas *qua* religious ideas have receded in importance, the cultural legacy of these ideas remains powerful.

The contributions of the early U.S. religious values to political consciousness are complex. Social historians, for example, have noted the strong sense of social obligation that existed in the Protestant communities of the New World.[5] These communities of the elect provided citizens the opportunity to incorporate Godliness in their daily lives, which included caring for each other. It is certainly not difficult, furthermore, to establish a scriptural basis for communitarian values, and the early Christian church was largely communitarian. As Bellah and his associates have shown, these values have survived and are important, but they are a minor theme in the development of the U.S. political culture.[6] Keeping this diversity and these pulls toward cooperation and community in mind, Protestantism nevertheless contributed to developing individualism in several important ways.

The United States always has been a religiously diverse society. The first amendment guarantees of religious freedom were not born out of a fear of religious intrusiveness. Some parts of colonial society were strongly theocratic. Rather, the first amendment was written out of a recognition that there was no consensus concerning which particular Protestant creed ought to dominate the culture. David Hackett Fischer[7] has shown that, even among British emigrants to the New World, there were four distinctive Protestant types. Perhaps the first contribution to individualism made by this religious tradition in America is the grudging, and it *was* grudging, acceptance of religious diversity.

There are also strongly individualist strains in the nature of Protestantism itself, however. Luther's rebellion against the church fundamentally reordered the relationship between Christians and their God. The Catholic Church has always served as an intermediary between God and lay Christians. The church hierarchy establishes the rules of Christian life, and the priest serves as an interpreter of these rules and an intercessor for the Christian. With Luther and the development of Protestantism the idea of hierarchy was seriously eroded, challenged by the notion of the priesthood of all believers. The access that Protestant Christians have to God is characteristically more immediate and personal. Protestants are far more likely to have intimate chats with God; Catholics to recite hierarchically sanctioned prayers.

Although there were Catholic emigrants to this country during the Colonial Period, overwhelmingly the religious folk coming from Europe were associated with the proliferating array of Protestant denominations. Since everyone was his own priest, it is hardly surprising that the number of Biblical interpretations began to multiply. Colonial society, backward in some respects, was astonishingly literate. This literacy was connected to burgeoning Protestantism,[8] as the ability to read was crucial to the lay understanding of God's will for individual lives. There were hierarchies in most Protestant groups during the Colonial period, but they were far flatter than the hierarchy of the Catholic Church. Furthermore, a disgruntled Roger Williams could leave a religiously stifling Massachusetts and start a society of his own in what has become Rhode Island. In short, Protestant churches elevated notions of individualism by their structure as well as by their theology.

The human condition, as it tended to be interpreted by various Protestant groups, also contributed to an individualist ethos. This condition is well summarized by the lengthy allegory, *Pilgrim's Progress*, written by the English Puritan, John Bunyan.[9] Aside from the Bible itself, Bunyan's book was the most widely read book in eighteenth-century America. Bunyan was not a writer given to subtlety, and he readily lays bare the human predicament: People are born in sin. All will one day be judged by God, according to their own merit. Most will be condemned to eternal damnation, but a few struggling Christians will, through a life of demonstrated devotion and resistance to the pulls of a sinful world, escape the wrath of God and enter the kingdom of heaven.

These religious ideas are still found in contemporary society, most obviously in fundamentalist groups. They undoubtedly serve to structure the political ideas of those who subscribe to such faiths. And although any Republican politician is well aware of the importance of these groups in current political life, culturally they are not ascendant. Today fundamentalists compete with a vast array of religious (and nonreligious) perspectives for the hearts and minds of the citizens. In today's world, the pilgrim's journey is more harrowing than even John Bunyan could have imagined.

If these ideas had been confined to a minority religious tradition, they would be less culturally significant than they are. The primary *cultural* significance of the ideas boldly outlined by Bunyan three hundred years ago is not that they are today *directly* expressed by a minority of the nation's religiously inclined. Rather, the significance rests in the fact that these religious ideas have been extended in secular form and have blended into the culture. Today they are accepted by millions of Americans who otherwise have little in common with the religious heirs of Bunyan. This secularization has been a continuous and complex historic process which can be marked by two prototypic representations.

Most Americans know of Ben Franklin, one of the nation's founders, but they know little about him. He is the balding, corpulent guy looking bemused on the front of a hundred-dollar-bill. He is most commonly regarded as a wise, genial kite-flyer, generally not considered one of especially great influence, in contrast to founders like Washington, Jefferson, or Madison. In part this is due to the politically unfortunate timing of his life. By the time of the Revolutionary and Constitutional periods, Franklin was well past his prime. He was treated with respect at the Constitutional Convention, but he contributed only marginally to its work. A further problem with taking Franklin seriously is that his philosophy is popularly revealed in an odd way—not as a systematic corpus, but in fragments contained in his autobiography and in the wildly popular *Poor Richard's Almanacks*. This annual anthology of information ranging from horticulture to philosophy was written and published by Franklin for twenty five years. The *Almanacks* were popular throughout the world (the *Almanack* essay "The Way To Wealth" was published in fourteen languages), but especially so in the colonies where it rivaled the Bible in popularity. The singular popularity of the *Almanacks*, in an age when print was the only medium, elevated Franklin to a position of cultural avatar.

Franklin is both a personal and philosophical embodiment of the secularization of the Puritan ethos that had been so dramatically expressed by Bunyan. He was raised in a strict Puritan home. In his autobiography[10] he reports that, aside from the Bible, *Pilgrim's Progress* was the first book he remembered reading. As an adult, Franklin gave up the Puritan faith and became a Deist. Nevertheless, important aspects of the Puritan ethic informed his public philosophy.

Franklin saw life as a struggle to prove one's worth. At one point, he noted all of his shortcomings as a human being and established a systematic plan in which, one by one, these would be eliminated. (He overlooked hubris.) The enemies one was likely to encounter along the road to self-improvement were similar to the enemies of Bunyan's Pilgrim, but they were more secularized: sloth, idleness, intemperance, debauchery, waste. The transformation represented by Franklin rests in the following: The Pilgrim lives a life of moral virtue in part by separating from the world. For Franklin these moral virtues become the keys to success in the business and social world the Pilgrim is counseled to eschew. A morality designed to make one worthy of an afterlife with God becomes, with a push from Franklin, a morality that will bring success in the mundane world. This advice he happily passed along in the *Almanacks*. "Be industrious and free," writes Franklin, "be frugal and free."

This is a significant transitional phase. Bunyan admonishes the pilgrim to stay apart from the world, advice conservative Protestants largely followed until they were redirected by televangelists Pat Robertson and Jerry Falwell in the 1970s. The secular world was designed to lure the weak away from the righteous path and to eternal damnation. Within the daily life of a colonial Puritan community, individual striving was tempered by a sense of social responsibility, as people sought to live godly lives. Franklin was a modern man who rejected the Puritan theology of his youth. His application of Puritan values was utilitarian. Yet his break with the Puritan tradition was not as clean as he may have imagined.

The second representational figure, Horatio Alger, follows Franklin by a hundred years. By the latter part of the nineteenth century, the Industrial Revolution had dramatically transformed the patterns of everyday life in America. Alger, the pious son of a Protestant minister, sought to marry the values of the older order to the brave new world people faced.[11] With the Industrial Revolution, the economic and social gap between the rich and the poor grew significantly, and the problem of rising and falling in the new society gained greater attention. Writing over one hundred success books that sold at least seventeen million copies, Alger emerged as one of the more formidable cultural arbiters of his day.

Like Bunyan, Alger was a moralist, not a novelist. The plot lines of his books are grindingly similar. Typically, they begin with a description of a street urchin who has many obvious faults but who is not fatally flawed in the way other (usually Irish) youth are. A chance encounter with some successful person causes the young hero to begin the struggle upward. He leaves the street, gets a watch, a new suit, becomes more mannerly, undertakes some useful education (but is not bookish), starts planning, and eventually rises into the respectable middle class. Most of his other friends from the streets, lacking the tenacity and discipline necessary for accomplishment, never make it out. They deserve their fates, just as the hero deserves his.

The Alger stories anticipate the profusion of self-help books that can be found in bookstores today. The theme remains enormously popular. The idea of self-improvement, of individual struggle, resonates through the contemporary culture. It is an old American fable, one rooted in the religious tradition that has been described. One scholar has noted that Alger is more nostalgic than progressive. Certainly there is little in his novellas to suggest great enthusiasm for the giant corporations that were emerging at the time he was writing. The captains of industry were enthusiastic about Alger's work because it provided a rationale for their legitimacy, but the Alger heroes never become capitalist giants. They do not rise "from rags to riches," the phrase that is attached to Alger's work. Rather, the Alger hero pulls himself out of the street into the respectable middle class. Alger *is* looking backward. He seeks to show that the fundamental values that were a part of his religious tradition could work in the brave new world of late nineteenth-century America.

Bunyan, Franklin, and Alger serve as useful benchmarks. Each contributes something fundamental in the cultural dynamics of individualism. Bunyan embodies the Puritan religious values that informed the consciousness of so many during the colonial period. Prominent among these values was the vision of life as a solitary journey in which the individual is responsible for his or her fate. As these values worked their way into the culture they became less explicitly religious, if not less fundamental. Ben Franklin serves to mark this transformation. Eventually these values were cut loose from their religious moorings altogether and placed in service of the emerging industrial order. Horatio Alger represents this phase of cultural adaptation. Although the great majority of Americans living today would not see themselves as religious Puritans, many subscribe to a secularized vision rooted in that tradition. For these, life remains an individual struggle to prove one's worth. They are not okay. They must succeed. They must "become."

INDIVIDUALISM AND THE U.S. REVOLUTION

Other factors were at work during the colonial period that also encouraged the development of individualism. Professor Gordon S. Wood, one of this nation's most distinguished historians, has argued in contrast to conventional wisdom, that the American Revolution was deeply radical.[12] It ushered in a new kind of popular politics, and for the first time made the interests and happiness of ordinary people the goal of government. To defend his thesis, Wood examines the hierarchical world challenged and ultimately shattered by the revolution.

The monarchical world view of eighteenth-century Europe was an important component of the culture of that time. As such, it ordered daily social relations. The monarchical world was one of personal dependencies, an organic world in which everyone had his or her place and everyone counted for something. Today most social connections are horizontal. People tend to associate according to different social classes. They work together, live in the same neighborhoods, go to the same kinds of churches, their children go to the same schools, and so forth. We may glimpse the lives of those in another class through television, or by taking the wrong turn off an interstate, but there is not much sense of people across classes being connected. Even ethnic groups have social class divisions within them.

In the pre-revolutionary, monarchical culture, people were connected vertically—but the connections were not of equals. They were connections of dependence and obligation. Patricians and plebeians were thought to have different natures, different psyches, even different physical characteristics. They were treated differently in law. The patriarchal family was the model for political and social relationships, and families were elaborate networks of kin and households, with patronage providing a binding web. Ordinary people accepted their lowly status as part of the natural order of things. The society was organic. Although the parts were unequal, each was seen as necessary to form the whole.

The monarchist world view dominated Europe. Of European nations, the British were the least committed to the monarchical ideal. The British in turn thought that their colonial brethren in America were poor monarchists. But Wood shows that even in America monarchical consciousness was quite strong through the 1750s. As pressure in America against this consciousness grew more intense, it strained, and ultimately ruptured. Wood sees the individualist logic of Protestantism as a key factor promoting this strain, but he identifies others as well. Rapid population growth and mobility also placed great stress on hierarchical social institutions such as households, churches, and neighborhoods. The increase in trade and the growing wealth of the average American stimulated an increase in consumerism. Ordinary citizens were able to acquire some of the goods formerly reserved for their "betters," which also weakened social hierarchy. The physical distance from the Old World encouraged independence as well.

As the colonies moved closer to armed confrontation with England, colonial leaders were placed in a difficult position. They needed to rally the population to the revolutionary cause. To do this, people had to be stirred, to feel that they had a vital stake in the outcome of the impending war. Liberal use of the rhetoric of freedom and democracy helped to stir these waters. This rhetoric was crucial to Thomas Jefferson's *Declaration of Independence,* to Tom Paine's widely circulated, revolutionary treatise *Common Sense,* to the clarion calls of the Sons of Liberty, and to the republican press of the day. Such public documents called into question an old order that had been eroding, and in so doing they escalated the process of erosion.[13]

After the war, the radicalism of the nation's leaders was tempered. The noble ideas expressed by Jefferson and Paine became more problematic. Progressive though they were for their times, many of the founders substantially distrusted the masses, and some have argued that the U.S. Constitution was in part an attempt to stem a rising democratic tide which was viewed with alarm in elite circles.[14] The nation's leadership was increasingly doubtful that ordinary citizens possessed sufficient republican virtue for self-government. Once the great democratic beast had been roused, however, it proved difficult to rein in. Wood reports that by the turn of the century many of the founders were quite depressed with the direction the society had taken and pessimistic about its prospects.

Wood shows that the radicalism of the American Revolution rested in its subversion of traditional hierarchies and establishing popular consent as the exclusive determinant of authority. "By the early nineteenth century, America had already emerged as the most egalitarian, most materialistic, most individualistic—and most evangelical Christian—society in Western history. In many respects this new democratic society was the very opposite of the one the revolutionary leaders had envisioned."[15] The revolution *was* a revolution. It undercut the hierarchical organicism that gave coherence to the old order. This coherence was dependent upon people knowing their place. The vanishing sense of place contributed to the flowering of individualism by allowing people to dream previously unimaginable dreams.

INDIVIDUALISM, SOCIAL MOVEMENT, AND SOCIAL MYTH

The existence of a frontier through the nineteenth century carried important cultural consequences. In contrast to older, more settled Europe, the United States engaged in long, continuous expansion through conquest and subjugation. For three hundred years, the frontier served as a constant reminder of renewal. This continuing frontier became a metaphor for interpreting the entire American experience, summarized by the phrase, "The Myth of the Frontier." For many, the idea of "starting anew" was not a theoretical abstraction, but a real possibility. White settlers were actively encouraged to migrate west, both by government policies which subjugated indigenous Indian and Mexican cultures and offered white settlers free land, and by private entrepreneurs interested in material gain.

Daily frontier life required a significant amount of social cooperation for survival.[16] Barn raisings, corn shuckings, quilting bees, and mutual protection served as explicit recognition of the benefits of cooperation. Yet in the American consciousness, the frontier came to be seen as the very expression of individualism. The frontiersman represented the individualist *par excellence*, a prime exemplar as well as a propagator of the culture.

The strength of individualism, well established by the time of Tocqueville's visit, is such that philosophic and social movements having individualist assumptions have always found a receptive American audience. Transcendentalism and self-reliance in the first half of the nineteenth century, Social Darwinism in the latter half of that century, and twentieth-century libertarianism have all enjoyed enthusiastic followings in the United States—much more so than in other nations. Taking root in a nurturing American soil, such movements have in turn served to reinvigorate the culture, presenting new variations of the individualist theme to accommodate changing social circumstances.

Heroic myths are common fodder in any culture, but heroic types vary. One indication of the importance of individualism is the central place it occupies in the mythic structure of the nation. The kinds of heroes that predominate in the American mythic pantheon conform to the tenets of individualism that have been discussed—in particular to its frontier aspects. By definition, the frontier exists at the border of "civilized" society, and it is therefore the place where social order and individualism may be most starkly juxtaposed.

The type of hero Americans most revere is the anti-hero—the solitary figure at best marginally connected to the social order. His heroism is in part embodied by stoical resolution, and his refusal to accept social integration. Often this is symbolized by the hero's inarticulateness—language being inherently social. He remains the outsider, often at the cost of his life, and thus sustains his integrity. To accept integration, the shared life of the community, is implicitly to court disaster. In folklore, the John Henry fable could well serve as the archetype. This black track layer for the railroad lines (he became white in some later versions of the story) had already established his separateness by his great physical capacity for work. His ultimate challenge is to outwork a steam drill, a metaphor for advancing technological society. The recalcitrant John Henry accepts the challenge and prevails, but at the cost of his life. Thus, John Henry was not integrated into the emerging order, but he remained a man unto himself, and therefore a man—and the stuff of legends.

A long line of similar heroes has been the staple of domestic cinema. Americans love the reluctant hero, the one who knows society is corrupt, who cannot live with its corruption, and who is therefore usually found somewhere on its social or geographical margins. Humphrey Bogart mined this mother lode early in cinematic history. Bogart's characters are found in Key Largo or Casablanca, on the Amazon or in the Sierra Madre, and their physical distance from society is paralleled by their psychic and social alienation. Reluctantly, they do the right thing, saving the society from the weaknesses of its ordinary members or from some monstrous enemy, but they return to the margin. This posture is similar to that of the roles played by the young Brando, James Dean, and dozens of would-be contemporary heirs.

In perhaps the most significant genre in American movies, the western, the John Henry fable provides *the* story line. *High Noon* is the classic case. Gary Cooper's sheriff must face a quartet of killers in a showdown. Initially the townsfolk are resolute in their support of the sheriff, knowing that the killers are bad news for the town, but as the fateful moment for the showdown draws closer, they one by one reveal their essential and snivelling cowardice, leaving the sheriff to face the bad guys alone. Even his bride deserts him, though she redeems herself at the last moment. When the hero prevails, the cowardly townsfolk emerge to congratulate him, whereupon the sheriff throws the symbol of his social connection, his badge, into the dirt and rides out of town with his contrite wife.

The basic structure of this plot can be seen in most westerns. The hero is typically the outsider, forever riding off into the sunset. Consider *Shane*, or *Pale Rider*, or virtually any John Wayne movie. Many other films have usurped this plot line and are really thinly disguised westerns. *Rambo*, *The Terminator*, and *Men in Black* are examples of this, as is the endless supply of cop-heroes. *Thelma and Louise* illustrates that the theme transcends gender, while *The Matrix* rockets it to the future. Dress up the story in a thousand ways. Tell it again and again. The appetite for it is unquenchable. The plot is so appealing to so many because it resonates so well with the culture.

One does not usually identify heroes of the American western with a religious tradition. They seem uncomfortable in church, which is normally portrayed as the province of women.[17] Yet the connections between the Western fable and early Puritanism are manifest. For the Puritan, as for the Western hero, the social order is dangerous and a source of corruption. These characteristics are inherent in society, which is why neither the pilgrim nor the hero can be at home there. At the conclusion of a western fable the hero rides off into the sunset, just as John Bunyan's hero, having survived the challenges of the earthly world, enters the gates of heaven. This world is not, nor was it ever, their home. John Wayne's use of the term "pilgrim" to describe fellow travelers in several of his films is not misplaced.

TECHNOLOGICAL ADAPTATION: THE EXAMPLE OF TV

As noted in Chapter One, cultures exist in the murky region between dynamism and stasis. The stability of cultures allows for the development of collective identity. At the same time, cultures adapt to new circumstance in order to survive. Technology, for example, is always introduced in a cultural context that will structure its elaboration and development. But technology also reorders possibility and restructures ways of seeing. This process can be seen with respect to individualism and one of the major technological innovations of the twentieth century, television.

Television has not only restructured what we do in this society, but also what we know. Most analysts believe that the average viewer spends twenty-five to thirty hours a week watching TV. Precise measurement is difficult because in a growing number of American homes TV sets are on as long as anyone is at home and awake. People do sit down in front of the tube for extended periods of time but, in addition, their attention drifts into and out of programs while they are doing other things. Because television is a constant presence in so many homes, determining the exact amount of time spent watching is probably impossible. What is clear is that America is a "TV Nation," and this has significant cultural implications. In Chapter Six, the role of television in promoting materialism will be considered. This chapter will highlight its connections to individualism.

It is possible to think of TV as a community-building technology—one that reduces the individualist tendencies of the culture. People watch a dramatic presentation and share their thoughts about it with co-workers the next morning. From the comfort of living rooms, people observe military actions in places like Bosnia. They are regularly invited to identify with a certain lifestyle through commodity purchase. The televised Super Bowl may be the closest thing Americans have to a national rite. People even become "friends" with TV personalities like Oprah Winfrey and Kathy Lee Gifford. In television's recast world, these things seem like the very stuff of community.

Whatever the community-building effects of television, the technology elevates individualism at a more basic level. As a visual medium, it is much better suited to conveying emotion and sentiment than it is to promoting rational discourse. Through the television, as Roderick Hart[18] has argued, characters are invited into living rooms. Such circumstances convey feelings of intimacy. On television, personality is central, ideas peripheral. The lines of fiction and nonfiction are blurred, even irrelevant. The sense of personhood is what matters. Ally, Jerry, Roseanne, and Frasier are known as personalities. So are Tom Brokaw and Sally Jessie's freaks. Dave and Jay are personalities who interview other personalities, all of whom are gorgeous or witty, and none of whom seems to have ever entertained an idea.

The dominant message of TV—that what is important in life is personality—extends the individualist dimensions of the culture. Beyond this message, the functional role of TV in American society, its *raison d'être*, also reinforces individualism. Put most simply, television is a vehicle for selling goods and services. Market transactions are by nature individual.

That is part of their attraction. Because the purpose of television is to move goods through the market, individualist appeals flood the airwaves. "You deserve a break today." "Treat yourself: you're worth it." "You can, yes you can, have it all." Commercial transactions are promoted by isolating individuals and placing them at the center of the universe—and by appealing to individual vanity and fears.

Finally, individualism is promoted by the structure of the television experience. If as much time is spent watching TV as experts claim, then it may be inappropriate to think of television as a "window to the world" or an ersatz environment. For many, television *is* the world, the "place" of interaction. And it is one that can be easily controlled. There are seventy-five channels. If one does not care for a particular environment, all one has to do is push a button. Sitting there on the sofa, the individual is part of the environment, but also rises above it, controlling it whimsically. "Don't tell me I need to think about Bosnia," the couch potato can muse. "I'm heading for Wheel of Fortune."

POLITICAL AND SOCIAL CONSEQUENCES OF INDIVIDUALISM

As one of the staples of the culture, individualism pervades the assumptions most Americans make about everyday experience, and shapes their shared sense of the world. The political and social consequences of this idea are therefore significant. Some of the more important of these will be identified in this concluding section of the chapter.

Historical memory is inextricably a part of collective identity. We come to understand who we are in part through knowledge of social history which tells us who we have been. Knowing history is problematic, however, because the number of facts that may be gleaned from historical experience are, in principle, infinite. History therefore awaits summation or, more precisely, interpretation. In a very real sense, the past is re-created in order to make life in the present more livable. Of course not all re-creations are equally plausible, and so there is a dialectic between past and present.

The individualist sensibility contributes to notions of history in at least two important ways. Most obviously, it structures the way the historical process is viewed. Americans tend to think of history as the story of great individual men and women doing things. Other generators of history, such as social processes and conditions, are downplayed, at least in popular consciousness. Attempts to bring such processes to the fore are met with resistance.

A less obvious but still significant consequence is that individualism denigrates the very idea of history. The evidence documenting the extraordinary ignorance that Americans have of their own history is abundant.

Many people cannot distinguish the Revolutionary from the Civil War—or even locate them in the correct centuries. Teachers frequently report the resistance of students to learning about "dead people." By placing the self at the center of society, immediacy is elevated. What matters is the present. Additionally, as previously noted, individualism minimizes the social imTORpediments to individual achievement. If such impediments are not significant, the point of learning history (beyond possible sources of personal inspiration) becomes obscure.

The American idea of progress as it relates to invention exemplifies the collective historical sense. Invention, discovery, and innovation are typically regarded as the function of isolated, great minds working autonomously. Thus people like Thomas Edison, Alexander Graham Bell, the Wright brothers, Henry Ford, and Jonas Salk are lionized. There is another way to think about the notions of invention and discovery, however. This alternative approach can be underscored by asking the question, "If Thomas Edison had never been born, would the world still be using kerosene lamps?"

Such a question highlights the community basis of invention and discovery. This is not to gainsay Edison's unique insight, but this insight would not have been possible without a history of discovery, insight, and disappointment that preceded him. Other pertinent questions might be considered as well. What was the role of Edison's family in providing the wherewithal for his time in the lab? How was he influenced by conversations with colleagues? How was he influenced by his educational experience? What were his sources of inspiration? The more one thinks about such questions, the more likely the discovery of electricity will be viewed differently. Perhaps Edison was the unique autonomous being of collective memory; on the other hand, perhaps that Edison is a social invention.

Individualism has an important impact on conceptions of politics. It influences the way issues are framed. Lyndon Johnson's biographers have noted how he personalized the Vietnam War, often referring to particular strategic decisions—such as an escalation in the bombing—in terms of the presumed effect that they would have on Vietnamese leader Ho Chi Minh personally. During the war in the Persian Gulf, George Bush did the same with Saddam Hussein. Deep historic grievances pertaining to the war were given minimal attention. Instead it was portrayed as the result of a madman, a new Hitler for a new generation.

The individualist ordering of reality had an impact on another recent American "war." President Reagan's famous "War on Drugs" was personalized in two ways. First, his administration argued that it was fundamentally linked to a corrupt authoritarian leader in Panama, General Manuel Noriega, who allowed drugs to be smuggled through his country into America. This argument was used as justification for the invasion of Panama and the capture and subsequent trial of General Noriega. Second, the war on drugs was personalized by portraying drug use as *merely* the function of individual choice. The problem of drugs would be eliminated if only individuals would "just say no," a phrase that became the anthem of the anti-drug campaign. But to frame issues in this way, as functions of individual responsibilities, is to depoliticize them.

It is possible to think about drugs in a political way by connecting drug usage to the allocative distribution of values. Perhaps poor people use drugs because their lives are so dreary that they seek pleasure wherever it can be found. Perhaps middle-class people use them because of the vacuity of their lives. Maybe people sell drugs because they provide the most reasonably available opportunity for economic advancement. Perhaps drugs should be legalized to eliminate the huge profit potential for criminal syndicates and the attendant crimes people commit to obtain the money to support their habits.

The foregoing are at least political ways to think about drugs and drug usage. They call into question patterns of social distribution. What Americans have instead is pseudopolitics: political puffery from posturing politicians working in a system which refracts the issue rather than taking it seriously. This posturing serves the interest of the social structure of power, as problems are interpreted in ways that do not threaten that structure. It is not surprising that today more drugs are coming through Panama than ever before, or that people don't "just say no." In lieu of having a serious conversation about drugs in this society, we settle for the only conversation the culture will allow, one larded with solemn but empty words and dubious solutions.

This example illustrates a more general point concerning individualism's effect on politics: its tendency to shade into self-absorption and to turn people away from the collective enterprise of politics. Tocqueville recognized this tendency 150 years ago. Individualism tends naturally to evolve into egoism. Of all the vices of the human heart, Tocqueville believed egoism served despotism best. His words have a remarkably contemporary ring:

> A despot will lightly forgive his subjects for not loving him, providing they do not love one another. He does not ask them to help him guide the state; it is enough if they do not claim to manage it themselves . . . he calls those "good citizens" who care for none but themselves.[19]

Tocqueville thought the young American society might successfully fend off this tendency because the founders wisely established a multilayered, federal system of government. The diverse array of political institutions, coupled with a vibrant voluntary associational life, would provide citizens a constant reminder of the public arena and instill in the population the habits of civic duty. He believed the negative tendencies of individualism could thus be averted. Today, given the unusually low levels of political interest and participation in this country, such optimism seems misplaced. Whatever the mitigating effects of federalism may have been, they have been overwhelmed by forces Tocqueville could not have anticipated.

Individualism encourages people not to think about politics. When citizens do think of politics, it encourages a distinctive turn of mind: the politics of acute egotism. As they turn to politics, citizens are encouraged to think of what is best for them or for some group with which they identify over the short term. Politics is about putting "me first," about grabbing all that one can for oneself. Early theorists of capitalism argued that the general welfare could best be maximized by each person thinking about how to promote his or her own private self-interests. If all pursued their self-interests this would also lead to the best outcomes for the society as a whole. When this happy theory was contradicted by experience, individualism encouraged the expansion of the American concept of politics from "me first" to "me first, screw them." With the evaporation of the idea that egoism leads to the collective good, egoism itself is not reconsidered. Rather, reality is redefined to conform to individualist assumptions, and one result is the feeding frenzy that annually occurs in the U.S. budgetary process.

The cultural value of individualism is pervasive enough so that political innovators have trouble mustering a vocabulary of opposition. Occasionally politicians will speak in the language of mutuality and community. Such language is crucial to policies like national health care and the national service corps. Usually, however, politicians use the more traditional political language of self-aggrandizement, and who can blame them? Opposing both entrenched economic interests *and* a political culture is very difficult.

There is much that is attractive about the value of individualism. Given the American experience, it is impossible to imagine it not being an important aspect of the way Americans define themselves. The impulse toward novelty seems to be part of human nature. An indomitable spirit, a willingness to struggle against odds, an enthusiastic optimism, can lead to exceptional accomplishment.

But it is also important to understand the limitations of individualism. It cannot be the root value of a culture because it cannot provide a solid foundation. A culture that suggests people gather together in order to be left alone borders on incoherence. It is an adolescent view, ultimately leading either to narcissism or to a state of war. Yet individualism does reside close to the core of the culture. It is constantly propagated in political and commercial rhetoric. Often it is described as freedom, by which most Americans mean nothing more than the absence of constraint—the ability to do one's own thing. This is an impoverished view of freedom, however. Such freedom is best obtained on a deserted island, but what kind of freedom is that? One is free to dine out, but where to go? One is free to read books, but who will have written them? One is free to hear music, but who will sing? Even the most fervent proponents of freedom are not looking for such places to live. A deeper sense of freedom is nurtured by mutuality and cooperation and thus, ironically, by constraint. A culture that values individualism must recognize that individualism inevitably emanates from shared lives and shared fates.

Cultures serve to simplify reality, helping to put together a suitable vision to be imposed on the world. A description of culture is a simplification of this simplification. In attempting to isolate a key component of the American identity, aspects of the culture that work against individualism have been inevitably downplayed. There is a communitarian strain within the Protestant tradition, for example, that rubs against individualism. Anyone who is reasonably attentive to American political and social life also knows that there are not only many generous people in the society, but also numerous examples of collective concern about others. Such countervailing forces mitigate the effects of pure individualism. In this society, however, these are minor (although important) aspects of our cultural tradition.[20] We shall return to these in the concluding chapter.

NOTES

1. Erving Goffman's *Asylums*, Chicago, IL: Aldine, 1962, is still one of the best treatments of this idea.
2. Isaiah Berlin, *Two Concepts of Liberty*, London: Oxford University Press, 1962.
3. Alexis De Tocqueville, *Democracy in America*, New York: Harper & Row, 1966, esp. Part II.
4. Garry Wills, *Under God*, New York: Simon and Schuster, 1990.
5. See for example Robert Bellah, et al., *Habits of the Heart*, Berkeley: University of California Press, 1985, and David Hackett Fischer, *Albion's Seed*, London: Oxford University Press, 1989.
6. Bellah, *op.cit.*.
7. Fischer, *op.cit.*
8. Fischer, *op.cit.*, especially part I.
9. John Bunyan, *Pilgrim's Progress*, Baltimore, MD: Penguin, 1965.
10. Benjamin Franklin, *Autobiography*, New York: Rinehart, 1959.
11. See Carol Nickenoff, *The Fictional Republic: Horatio Alger and American Political Discourse*, New York: Oxford University Press, 1994.
12. Gordon S. Wood, *The Radicalness of the American Revolution,* New York: Vintage, 1993.
13. For a compelling account of the republican press of the Revolutionary and Constitutional periods, with extensive inclusion of primary sources, see Richard Rosenfeld's *American Aurora*, New York: St. Martin's Press, 1997.

14. See for example Michael Mezey, *Congress, the President, & Public Policy*, Boulder, CO: Westview Press, 1989, and Richard N. Rosenfeld, *op. cit.*

15. Wood, *op.cit.*, p.230.

16. Garry Wills, *Reagan's America*, New York: Doubleday, 1987.

17. Jane Tompkins, *West of Everything*, London: Oxford University Press, 1992.

18. Roderick P. Hart, *Seducing America,* London: Oxford University Press, 1994.

19. Tocqueville, *op. cit.*, p.481.

20. See Bellah, et al., *op. cit.*

4

The Game of Life

It must be emphasized . . . that competitiveness, and the potential hostility that accompanies it, pervades all human relationships. . . . It must be added, however, that this rivalry itself is not biologically conditioned but is a result of given cultural conditions, and furthermore, that . . . the competitive stimuli are active from the cradle to the grave.

—Karen Horney

In 1888 Edward Bellamy published his famous social critique, the utopian novel *Looking Backward*. In it, the narrator is hypnotized and falls into a deep sleep. He awakens in the year 2000, by which time America has escaped the turbulence of the late nineteenth century and has evolved into a perfect society. The novel presents a series of dialogues between the narrator and his twenty-first century host, who explains the virtues of the "new" America and how the transition occurred. Through the character of the host, Bellamy argues that the main impediment to perfection was selfish cultural and economic competition. When cooperation replaced competition as the governing social ethic, perfection became possible.

Such is the way of fiction. If Bellamy himself could be revived like the narrator of his story, he would be keenly disappointed. America in 2000 is far from the society of which he dreamed. While he might recognize some new evidence of cooperation, competition has hardly been transcended. In many ways it has been extended.

The historian Gordon Wood notes a growing sense of competition in the earliest days of the Republic.[1] But although the idea of competition antedates the Industrial Revolution, it was the maturing industrial era that elevated it to a principle of social organization. In industrial society, the consequences of competition were much more keenly felt, magnified by the inflated stakes of winning and losing. The nineteenth century ended with levels of economic inequality that would have been unimaginable to citizens who witnessed that century's birth. Outraged by this inequality, Bellamy placed much of the blame on runaway competition.

Like individualism, competition is both a major and a distinctive strut of American culture. Each of these values reinforces the other. In the previous chapter, we saw how individualism calls self-worth into question. In consequence, outperforming others becomes a way to buttress flagging self-esteem. On the other hand, we shall see that competition serves to drive people apart, which reinforces individualism. In his definitive assessment of competition in America, Alfie Kohn argues that our devotion to this norm exceeds that of any other society.[2] Kohn's conception of competition will be used to frame our observations. In his study, competition is characterized by mutually exclusive goal attainment. This means that one's success requires another's failure. Competition may be structural— that is, embedded in the objective situation itself, as in a game. It may also be intentional—or rooted in an individual's proclivity for beating others, regardless of the situation. A party, for example, is not inherently competitive, but someone can make it so by trying to show he is the most intelligent person there.

By defining competition as mutually exclusive goal attainment, Kohn seeks to rule out what some call "competing with oneself." For Kohn, this phrase is an oxymoron. At bottom, competition is interactive. Thus, competition is more integral to some forms of athletics than to others. Tennis and most team sports are characterized by mutually exclusive goal attainment, as the success of one is inherently connected to the failure of another. On the other hand, a sport like track and field is more ambiguously competitive. In one sense, the point is to win a race, and to that extent the sport is competitive. But it is quite possible for a runner to finish last in a race and to feel elated if she ran her fastest time. The rewards of self-improvement or the measurement against some external standard are different from the rewards of winning. Americans tend to see competition as a necessary condition for striving and doing well. This chapter describes the nature of this view, considers how it has risen to prominence, and indicates some of its political and social consequences.

COMPETITION AND THE CONVENTIONAL WISDOM

There are a number of assumptions about competition that Americans broadly share. These assumptions are reinforced and extended in everyday experience, and they will arise in almost any conversation about competition. One of these is that *competition is natural*. Often, this assumption about competition is also used to ratify it: Competition is seen as good simply *because* it is natural. Others argue that this natural human propensity confers benefits both to individuals and to society as a whole. One of these benefits, and the second broadly shared assumption about competition, is that it *builds character*, and therefore makes us better people. Third, competition is viewed as the *midwife of progress*. It contributes to individual progress, essential in a society that also values social mobility. It is also held that competition leads to collective progress as well—to the improvement and advancement of society. Each of these assumptions deserves elaboration.

Americans commonly believe that competing is part of human nature. Thus, to suggest that competition is cultural—that is, a socially-constructed norm—will immediately invoke skepticism. In the dominant American view, human history can largely be read as an ongoing, competitive struggle. Furthermore, competition is not merely confined to our species. It is part of the larger order of things, a characteristic humans share with other animals—and with plant life as well—as the struggle for the scarce resources necessary for survival unfolds. The frequently used admonition "It's a jungle out there!" conveys precisely this competitive sense of the social world of everyday experience. It recognizes that society never strays too far from the natural order, where it is eat or be eaten, and the real Golden Rule is "Do unto others before they do unto you." Life is competitive, a game of winners and losers, and for this reason few epithets carry a sharper bite than "loser."

In the latter half of the nineteenth century an ideology based upon this sense of congruence between the social and natural world emerged, and it is instructive that Social Darwinism, as it was called, found its most receptive audience in the United States.[3] This ideology sought to deduce social principles from Charles Darwin's revolutionary treatise on the natural world, *The Origin of Species*, published in 1860. Darwin's great insight was his recognition that organisms were integrally connected to their environments. They adapted to them, in a natural process. In an arid climate, for example, those representatives of particular species needing less water lived longer. Therefore, they produced more offspring than those representatives lacking this characteristic. Over time, this process of "natural selection" extended the trait of low water need throughout the entire species. Those who were "most fit" for survival in their environment had survived. Any species that could not adapt would die off.

The Origin of Species generated great excitement in the scientific community and in broader intellectual circles as well. Most familiar is the response of some religious leaders who, accustomed to the idea of a more direct hand of God in the act of creation, saw the work as heretical. However, the book also interested others who were seeking to explain the emerging social order. The Englishman, Herbert Spencer, extracted organizing social principles from Darwin's observations of the natural world. Not especially popular in his native country, Spencer was celebrated in America. In the latter half of the nineteenth century, 368,755 copies of Spencer's books were sold here, extraordinary for dense academic tomes on the subjects of philosophy and sociology. Richard Hofstadter notes that Spencer's philosophy was well-suited to late nineteenth-century America.[4] It had the patina of science, which was beginning a long period of intellectual ascendancy. It buttressed the theory of progress, central to the American experience, and based it upon biology and physics. And it seemed particularly well-suited to interpret the fierce competition that had emerged in this young industrial society.

Even before the publication of Darwin's work, Spencer had been distressed by England's drift toward state intervention in the economy. Aspects of Darwin's thought became the foundation for his comprehensive social philosophy promoting laissez faire. It was Spencer, not Darwin, who coined the term "survival of the fittest." Spencer believed that state intervention violated the natural order because it propped up inefficiencies and therefore retarded progress. Thus, state aid to the poor was pernicious because it weakened the species by artificially supporting those who could not naturally compete.

Social Darwinism extended the imprimatur of science to the extraordinary social position of the new industrial elite in America, and Spencer was warmly received by this class. He was frequently feted by "captains of industry" such as John D. Rockefeller and Andrew Carnegie. Carnegie was a particularly devoted enthusiast, and his own very popular book, *The Gospel of Wealth*, published in 1900, is based upon Social Darwinist principles. In Carnegie's book, the idea of competition evolved into "the law of competition," and thus was accorded the status of natural law. Competition had its costs, but its benefits—material development—were more than compensating. This "law" allowed Carnegie to assume that he and his friends were the most deserving in the society. They had won, and to the victors go not only the spoils, but also the responsibility of social and moral leadership.

Social Darwinism was hardly an uncontested philosophy. It was vigorously opposed by critics such as Lester Ward, and by a variety of social movements emerging in that turbulent time.[5] Vestiges of Social Darwinism can still be found in some conservative and libertarian circles, but today most Americans are unwilling to accept the more draconian implications of its logic. Social Darwinism has, nevertheless, left its imprint on American culture. It is still commonly used in popular discourse to frame issues. Its greatest legacy is the broadly shared conviction that competition is inevitable and eternal. Humans cannot escape biology. We may be a special sort of animal, but we are, in the end, animals.

Americans also tend to believe that competition is not only natural, but good. Therefore, it should be nurtured and institutionally reinforced. The relationship between the culture of competition and the institutions arising in that culture is dialectical: Institutions assume the mantle of competition and also serve to reinforce and extend it. Darwinian metaphors permeate the world of work. Downsizings are justified by the view that economic institutions are locked in a deadly competitive struggle and must do what is necessary to survive. Antitrust laws grow out of a belief in the necessity of maintaining competition. Individuals in the workplace see themselves as competitors, not simply with rival businesses, but with colleagues in this "dog-eat-dog" world, as they battle for individual recognition and promotion. In marketing products, businesses stimulate competitive urges in consumers as a way to increase sales.

The idea of competition is not only promulgated by the economic institutions of society. American religious institutions exhibit a competitive dimension as well. Often religion is seen as a zero-sum game, where the advancement of one faith means the diminution of another. Eschatologies promote the ultimate competition, a final battle between the forces of good and the forces of evil. Numbers are kept and regularly reported indicating which denominations are growing and which are not. Evangelists distribute press releases, announcing the number of "souls won to Christ." This competition was highlighted in 1998, when Southern Baptists, the largest Protestant denomination in the United States, decided to hold their annual meetings in Salt Lake City, mecca of the Church of Jesus Christ of Latter Day Saints—more commonly known as Mormons. Baptists and Mormons are both major zero-sum players, and during this week the streets of Salt Lake were filled with duelling representatives of the two faiths, each trying to convert the other.

Schooling in America is highly competitive also. Some education professionals, recognizing the value of cooperation in the acquisition of knowledge, struggle to resist this trend by introducing cooperative activities in the classroom, but these are overwhelmed by broader tendencies. Grading is inherently competitive. Children are constantly aware of the consequences of failing to outperform their classmates. Bumper stickers proudly boast of children who are "honor students" at Tidy Didey Classical College Prep Elementary School. Parents delay the entry of their children into the school system in order to give them competitive advantage over younger classmates. Graded tracking systems promote the ethic of competition and socialize students to it. One elementary public school in Chicago, for example, has four tracks for their students. Administrators live in fear of school rankings that result from comparative standardized examinations. Some families spend $25,000 and more in private programs designed specifically to boost their children's scores on ACT and SAT examinations. High school students develop elaborate resumés, less because of the intrinsic value of any particular activity than to increase their competitive advantage in college admissions. Such admission is regarded, in turn, as a ticket to the right graduate school or job.

The world of sport also serves to promote the idea of competition. Whether as spectator or participant, the point is increasingly, and now overwhelmingly, to win—to experience the thrill of victory as opposed to the agony of defeat. Americans love to chant, "We're Number One!" Being Number Two will not do. Athletes whose main distinction is their competitive zeal are lauded and promoted as "role models" for children. Slogans glorifying the importance of victory are used to market athletic equipment. In childhood, autonomous play is being eclipsed by organized sport, as adults establish competitive leagues for children not yet in kindergarten. Often such leagues seem benign. When children are young, their parents talk predominantly about simply having fun. Over time, as parents constantly urge maximum effort from the sidelines, berate and sometimes even assault referees and umpires, the kids can hardly miss the point: to win. Politicians, business executives, religious leaders, educators, and others use competitive sports metaphors to frame issues and problems. In this milieu, life *is* a game, and a competitive one at that.

The cultural characteristic of competition is thus promoted and extended by many of the institutions through which Americans live their daily lives. It is also eagerly promoted by parents, coaches, teachers, and other authority figures. Competition is extended because it is believed to build character, honing the skills necessary for success. It prepares us for the "real world," and therefore makes us better people. Mia Hamm and Michael Jordan duking it out on the playing field, neither willing to concede that the other is better, are held up for admiration and emulation. No one summarized this attitude better than Army General Douglas MacArthur, who fifty years ago addressed cadets during half time of an Army–Navy football game:[6] "On these fields of friendly strife are sown the seeds that, on other fields, in other days, will yield the fruits of victory." Thus, competitive games are not just fun. They instill the "right stuff" and prepare us for the more serious tasks which lie ahead.

Finally, Americans venerate competition because they believe it stimulates progress—both for the individual and for society as a whole. Two students aspire to be the top student in a math class. Only one can succeed, but as each struggles to achieve this end, both become better math students than they would have been without the competition. A child becomes a better writer because of the incentive to win a Young Authors contest. Such putative benefits of competition are widely touted, and not just for individuals. Without competition, it is believed, the incentive for self-improvement is sharply diminished. The benefits of competition are especially promoted in business theory. Thus, IBM and Macintosh want to sell personal computers. In order to do so, they compete with each other in a variety of ways. Each may try to make comparable PCs more cheaply than the other. Or they may struggle to introduce attractive innovations in their line. In this competitive struggle PCs get better or prices go down, or both. No matter what, competition is good for the consumer. The federal government's suit against Microsoft was based on the fear that the company was stifling competition and hence hindering progress.

Most people recognize that it is possible to be too competitive, but because competition is so integral to our culture, it is hard to figure out why it may be a problem. It organizes, frames, and interprets experience and so we promote it. We are ecstatic when our favorite team wins a national championship. Applications for admission to universities soar when they have athletic success. We want to be known as winners. At the same time, most people will decry instances of competition "going too far." It is important to recognize, however, that instances of "excessive" competition are not aberrations. Typically, they follow from the logic of competition itself. A culture that is so overwhelmingly focused on the virtue of competition obscures its harmful effects, some of which work against the attainment of the supposed ends of competition itself. The problematic features of competition can be seen by assessing the assumptions that underlie the cultural support for it.

THE CONVENTIONAL WISDOM ASSESSED

Several things might be considered in response to the argument that competition is natural to human beings because it pervades the natural world. In the first place, not all "natural" characteristics deserve to be nurtured. All societies generate rules that repress impulsive behavior, though these rules vary from society to society. Systems of ethics, manners, and the like seek to repress socially undesirable forms of behavior. Sigmund Freud is only one of many to recognize that civilization requires the repression and sublimation of some basic human drives.[7] Accepting competition as natural does not in itself justify its encouragement.

Additionally, although humans are animals, it is crucial to understand what kind of animal the human being is. It is possible, after all, that a quality relevant to a large portion of the animal kingdom does not extend to all because of the substantial variation within that kingdom itself. Several human qualities are relevant to these considerations. One is the overwhelming evidence of human sociability. Recall Aristotle's dictum that humans are "social animals." Everywhere one finds people, one finds them in groups. Exceptions are so rare that they are not worth discussing. It is possible that competition is a motive for human sociability, that we live together in order to prove ourselves better than others. This is a very weak thread with which to bind civil society, however, as it defies both credibility and evidence. The ubiquitous social instinct grows out of a profound human need—one might say out of a profound need to be human. Because humans need each other, we are overwhelmingly cooperative.

This recognition seems strange in a culture that emphasizes both the naturalness and the virtue of competition. Instances of cooperation are missed because they are so ordinary and so overwhelming. In contrast, competition stands out, even in a society that promotes it. Consider the extraordinary level of cooperation required in the simple act of traveling on an interstate highway. Drivers change lanes, merge, regulate their speeds, enter and exit for the most part seamlessly and cooperatively. Indeed, interstate travel would be impossible were it not so. A significant number of motorists, however, turn driving into an act of intentional competition, darting in and out of traffic and in other ways seeking to defeat "rival" drivers. It is reasonable to attribute this behavior partly to the competitiveness of U.S. culture, but to conclude that it reflects natural instincts is not reasonable. The behavior is noticeable precisely because it is extraordinary.

A second human characteristic relevant to this discussion is that, far more than any other species, humans live in an environment that they themselves have made. In Chapter One we noted that Kenneth Burke identifies this as a defining characteristic of our species. Habitually, persistently, humans reconstruct physical and symbolic environments. Thus, the problem with all "state of nature" arguments with respect to human beings is finding evidence that they have ever been there. It is the built environment that archaeologists offer as evidence of human life. Wherever one finds humans, one finds environments that have been both physically and spiritually reconstituted. This means that environments can be built which are more, or less, competitive, and both history and contemporary anthropology amply record this variation.[8] Perhaps a highly competitive environment is desirable, but this is not so because it is natural.

Third, the distinctive moral capacity of human beings is also relevant to these considerations. Humans do not simply act in the world, they also think about their actions. They argue about what is fair, what is just, the nature of a good life. There is no evidence to suggest that a lion thinks about what is good for a springbok when the lion is hungry. It does not think about competition, or social justice, or right living. Humans do have such thoughts, as animal rights activists and vegetarians will readily attest. This capability enables us to consider the effects of competition in a way that is beyond the capacity of other species in the animal kingdom.

For these reasons, identifying human and animal behavior is a dubious enterprise, and very often anthropomorphic. The animal kingdom can be summoned to bestow legitimacy on a wide array of contradictory human behavior. It can be argued, for example, that the animal kingdom exhibits more of the human quality of cooperation than it does of competition. It should be remembered that phrases like "It's a jungle out there," "It's kill or be killed," and so forth are not proffered as advice on the appropriate way humans should treat chickens. These aphorisms are meant to provide instruction on what to expect from fellow humans, through analogies to the natural world. In the animal kingdom writ large, however, "competition" within species to which such aphorisms refer is comparatively rare, and even interspecies "cooperation" is more common than competition. This interdependence grows out of Darwinist needs for survival. Kohn reviews a wealth of biological and zoological research documenting this reality.[9] The argument that the natural world is fundamentally competitive imputes an allegedly "natural" characteristic to the animal kingdom what is in fact a cultural characteristic of the society.

There is, furthermore, an important distinction to be made between Darwinism and Social Darwinism. Charles Darwin sought simply to describe the process through which species adapted and survived over time. In this sense, it was devoid of moral content. Social Darwinists, in contrast, were highly moralistic. They equated laissez faire capitalism with nature itself and sought to freeze that particular social order in time, requiring people to adapt to it. Policy makers proposing ameliorative social programs were scolded by Social Darwinists for violating natural law. Such posturing makes little sense to those who observe natural selection in the animal kingdom. In a moral sense, Darwin's ideas are almost tautological: Whatever creatures have survived, and however they have done it, they are the most "suited" to survive. But Social Darwinists have a survival agenda. People ought not to survive by making claims on elected officials, or by forming labor unions, because such things violate the supposed natural order. It is as if Darwin were to vilify ants because they enhance their survivability by forming colonies.

Finally, the fact that competition varies so substantially across cultures is problematic for the belief that it is natural. Anthropologist Margaret Mead's study of Samoan society offered decisive evidence against this belief.[10] This variation has been documented by other anthropologists as well. Competition largely seems to be a product of western industrialized systems, but even within these systems there is significant variation. This suggests that, rather than being natural, competition is learned. As a learned phenomenon, we can understand why the United States exists at the far end of the competition–cooperation spectrum. It is something in which we receive extensive education.

Although the supposed "naturalness" of competition weighs heavily in the arguments of those who support it, the case for or against competition does not ultimately depend upon whether it is a universal genetic predisposition. It may be a good thing, even if it is not natural. One of the additional claims about competition is that it builds character, in the manner so cogently summarized by General MacArthur.

This argument involves some intellectual sleight-of-hand. Certainly any pervasive human activity is likely to affect development, and hence to build character. But character building is a neutral process. There are characters and then there are characters. An abusive childhood builds character, too. We cannot simply assume that the kind of character construction encouraged by competition is positive, and we must therefore consider carefully the character competition nurtures. To see this clearly, it is important to focus upon the essence of competition.

Perhaps the most certain quality of character to which competition contributes is that it makes people more competitive. This is the immediate meaning behind General MacArthur's comments, which argue that playing football prepares us for the ultimate form of competition: warfare. Whether this is a good thing is an open question. Most of us do not find a competitive personality to be particularly attractive in others, even though we may praise the idea of competition in an abstract sense. Moreover it seems that the more competition is elevated as an ideal, the more important winning becomes, the greater the likelihood of unattractive character development. This is because the logic of competition works against the development of qualities that detract from the objective of winning.

Consider the kinds of persons you admire in your everyday life—as opposed to the "role models" constantly being promoted in mass media advertisements. What qualities do these people possess? We tend to admire those who have a strong sense of who they are, who have ethical systems that are meaningful to them, and who are kind, considerate, and empathic. We also like people who have a nice sense of humor, including the ability to laugh at themselves.

Competition works against such qualities. The more important winning becomes, the greater the pressure to repress them. Because competition is very serious business, it encourages the dehumanization of others, and subsumes ethical standards to the all important task of winning. The more intense the competition, the greater the urge to ignore ethical standards and values that are independent of the competitive frame. The highly successful professional football coach, Vince Lombardi, is reputed to have said, "Winning isn't everything; it's the only thing." (Whether he actually said this or not is irrelevant. It is part of his legend, and is held up for admiration.) But if this is the case, then character traits not conducive to winning must be suppressed, and those that are, promoted.

Intercollegiate athletics illustrate how competition tends to edge out other values that are normally admired. So important has winning become at some universities that a coach can be more powerful than the president of the university. Coaches who do not win are dismissed, regardless of what other qualities they may bring to their jobs. Under competitive pressures, rules are bent or broken to admit athletes to school and keep them eligible. Coaches often lie to players, telling them they have a chance for a pro contract if they dedicate themselves singularly to their sport. Unable to devote time to academics, athletes are herded into courses taught by professors who are themselves so enamored of the athletes that they will pass them no matter what. Sometimes athletes are encouraged to cheat in order to remain eligible for sports. Others are pushed off teams to free a scholarship slot for a more promising player. Alumni ply athletes with favors to keep them happy. To elicit maximum effort in the competitive struggle, opponents are regularly dehumanized and turned into objects of hatred. Fans ride opposing players mercilessly, sometimes using racist and sexist epithets, in an attempt to increase the competitive advantage for their team. A few years ago, hatred between the University of Miami and Notre Dame became so intense that it was necessary to suspend football games between the two schools.

These things are all logical extensions of the elevation of competition as a cultural value, and they apply not only to athletics but wherever this value predominates. It is worth stressing that, although the things described in the paragraph above are prevalent, they are not universal. There are many honorable coaches, players, athletic administrators, and even a few honorable fans. To the extent that this is the case, however, it is because the temptations of competition have been resisted. Some, swimming against the tide, affirm that winning is *not* the only thing. To do this, they rely on standards that exist outside the realm of competition. They also reduce their chances of winning.

Even though competition may not be natural, and even though it may not build admirable character, it may still be justified if it promotes individual and social progress. Thus, the proponents of competition argue that it generates the incentive to perform better. The desire to win, or the fear of losing, stimulates a struggle to improve, with resulting benefits both for the individuals involved and for society as a whole. It was competition, ultimately, that produced Mark McGwire's home run records, and it was competition with the Soviet Union that propelled the United States into space.

The idea that competition leads to individual and social progress is so widely accepted that it is rarely assessed. On the contrary, its motivational significance is constantly reinforced in everyday life. We are so comfortable with this idea that its truth seems self-evident. Part of this certainty about the virtue of competition may be a function of "seeing-that" discussed in Chapter One.[11] Americans may be so used to "seeing-that" competition stimulates progress that there is little reason to question whether or not it really does. There are many things beyond the competitive frame that might motivate a Mark McGwire or a desire to go into space. Furthermore, the struggle for improvement is only one of the outcomes generated by competition. This outcome is perhaps most visible because in a competitive situation attention is constantly drawn toward winners. To assess competition as a cultural phenomenon, however, we must consider its main effects.

That competition stimulates progress seems self-evident in the experience of everyday life, making systematic verification unnecessary. However, in the social science community, there has been a significant amount of research on the effects of competition on achievement. Much of the impetus for this work originated in the field of education, as researchers have tried to figure out how to improve national education performance. The research has extended to other areas as well, however. Two things are surprising about this work. The first is that the results of it are unidirectional. Various studies in a variety of fields point to a single conclusion. The second surprise of this work, given the context of U.S. culture, is the conclusion itself: Competition is not an effective stimulus to achievement.

In the field of education, perhaps the most significant work has been done by brothers David and Roger Johnson. Along with a research team from the University of Minnesota, they have conducted a variety of studies assessing different classroom learning environments. For our purposes, their most useful report is a meta-analysis including their own work as well as research conducted by others. In all, 122 studies throughout North America on the effects of various goal structures on student achievement were compared and contrasted.[12] In these studies, three learning environments were evaluated: cooperative environments, in which students worked together to accomplish tasks; competitive environments, in which students competed against each other; and individualistic environments, in which students worked independently. The results of this meta-analysis are striking. While the study found no significant differences between individualistic and competitive learning environments on student achievement and productivity, it showed that cooperation was substantially superior to both. These results hold for all subject areas, and for students in age groups ranging from elementary school through college. In some classroom settings, there was cooperation *within* groups but competition *between* groups. Interestingly, students in such settings ranked in the middle in achievement and productivity. They did better than students in purely competitive environments but not as well as students in purely cooperative environments.

Research has not been limited to students in the classroom. One study of academic psychologists revealed results similar to those of the Minnesota research group.[13] Using a specially designed Work and Family Orientation Questionnaire (WOFO), the researchers generated three scales of motivation. The "Work Orientation" scale measured the desire to work hard and to do a good job. The "Mastery" scale measured a preference for challenging tasks and for meeting internally prescribed standards for performance. The "Competitiveness" scale measured the enjoyment of interpersonal competition and the desire to win and be better than others.

A sample of academic psychologists were asked a series of questions about their work motivations. These answers located the respondents on each of the three scales. They were then rated according to their research productivity. Research productivity was measured by the number of publications a person had, and the number of times his or her work was cited by other researchers—a commonly accepted measure of prestige in academia. The most productive scholars were those who ranked high on the Work and Mastery scales but low on the Competitiveness scale. These relationships held for both relatively young scholars and for those who were well along in their careers.

Using the same WOFO Scale, researchers examined other social spheres.[14] In one study, 1300 college students were located on these scales during their first year of college. Two years later, researchers matched these results against cumulative GPA. The same trends held. Predictably, students scoring low on all three scales had the lowest GPAs. Students whose GPAs were highest scored high on the Work and Mastery scales, but low on the Competitiveness scale. This group did better than those scoring high on all three scales.

Surprisingly, these findings held in a study of businessmen where, once again, interpersonal competitiveness was negatively related to attainment. This study measured annual salary and controlled for years of postgraduate experience. Those businessmen scoring high in work–mastery but low in competitiveness earned more than their competitive peers and were the best paid of all the groups.

Examples of this kind of empirical research could easily be extended, and are unambiguous. Competition typically does not encourage productivity; on the contrary, it is usually negatively associated with it. Why should this be the case? A wise statistics professor in graduate school once advised our class that when statistical data violated what was intuitively plausible, one should doubt the data. We have here an evident example of data contradicting common sense. It seems intuitively plausible that competition would lead to productivity and progress, but does it? Actually the results of these studies are quite reasonable, and only confound us because we are culturally conditioned to think competition is productive. There is good reason to believe that, in fact, it is this cultural trait that is strange.

Any competition produces a loser as well as a winner, and the competitive frame produces far more losers than winners. Only one team can win the Super Bowl. Certainly there are those who argue that losing also builds character and teaches valuable lessons. However, these lessons can only be learned because of values existing outside the competitive frame. The point of competition is to win. Those who do not win, fail. The greater the significance of the competitive frame as a transmitter of social values, the greater the importance of winning and the greater the ignominy of defeat. Professional basketball's Karl Malone and the Utah Jazz, who exist in that rarefied atmosphere reserved for extraordinary athletes, are more recognized for "failing to win the big one" than for accomplishment. Losing, in other words, is painful.

People do not like pain. One of the inefficiencies of competition, therefore, will be that many, rather than facing defeat, will opt out of a competitive situation. They will thus fail to reach their potential. As Homer Simpson advised son Bart, who had just confronted failure, "You've tried and you've failed. The lesson here is, *never* try." This is clearly seen in the educational tracking system, theoretically designed to group students according to "abilities." Students assigned to the slow track are almost impossible to teach, for quite understandable reasons. They have been told by the system that they are stupid. In consequence, the education system is the last place to which they are likely to turn for accomplishment. Even the best teachers will be overwhelmed by the structural realities of the competitive tracking system. Similarly, everyone would physically benefit from athletic endeavor, but many drop out of athletics altogether because the emphasis upon competition makes them feel inadequate.

Another inefficiency of competition is that it encourages information hoarding. If the point is to win, why would people want to share helpful information with competitors? This means that not only are students and workers less likely to learn from each other, but also that there is a tangible reason to keep others from learning. The education system is replete with evidence of this type of inefficiency. Some students resent giving notes to those who have missed class, while others cut key articles out of journals, or hoard books. Many are reluctant to share knowledge of how to solve a problem to protect their competitive advantage. That in the real world the values of friendship and generosity lead many students to share information happily should not obscure the tendencies that competition itself encourages.

One researcher who has studied competitive situations has suggested that competition may also be inefficient because it detracts from the real task, which is doing well.[15] People may get so wrapped up in winning that they look for shortcuts to their goals. College entrance examinations offer a good example of this kind of inefficiency. Conceived as standardized ways to predict student success in college, the ACTs and the SATs were originally means to an end.[16] The idea was that they would reflect the hard work and aptitude of potential students. Competition has led to an increasing focus on the exams as ends in themselves, however. Class time is now used to help students prepare for them. Those whose families can afford it often take classes or obtain other private instruction on how to ace the exams. Such classes commonly have units on the logic of multiple choice questions and question phrasing, statistical tendencies in the exams, and so forth. These things may help students improve their scores and therefore increase their competitive advantage, but educationally they are distractions. Students may end up doing better and knowing less.

Finally, competition can lead to resentment which also generates inefficiency. Winners may be admired, but they are also envied and resented. A winner must be very careful because of the damage that has resulted as a consequence of the competitive situation. Our fixation on the idea of "role models" underscores this resentment. By definition, winners are "better" than the rest of us, and so they are expected to be role models—meaning that they should not have much fun. They are watched carefully for evidence of weakness, and few things are more exciting than seeing the mighty getting their comeuppance.

Competition alienates competitors from each other. In general, the more intense the competition, the greater the alienation. This can be illustrated by considering the most extreme form of competition—warfare. Since warfare requires killing, and as such runs contrary to our natures as social and moral beings, it exacts a huge psychological toll on its participants. In order to kill, therefore, soldiers must be distanced from the enemy. The enemy must become an "other," even subhuman. In the 1991 war with Iraq, Saddam Hussein became the new "Adolph Hitler" according to President George Bush; Bush became the "Great Satan" according to Hussein. In longer hot and cold wars, propaganda films depict enemy nations and leaders as the quintessence of evil. Enemy soldiers are dehumanized. They become Krauts, Gooks, Japs, and Wops. Such epithets, unacceptable in more civil times, are tolerated because of the requirement of dehumanization.

As an extreme form of competition, war highlights competition's effects, but the process of social distancing is evident in all forms of competition. The term "friendly competition" is deceptive, for competition is never friendly. What this term actually means is that norms outside the competitive frame will regulate and control the competition itself. The more intense the competition, the greater the urge to dehumanize. Anger toward an opponent extends athletic effort. Coaches peruse sports pages for quotes from an opponent that can be interpreted as insulting. This phenomenon is underscored by recognizing that despised "enemy" players immediately become objects of adoration when they join the local franchise.

If competition is in many ways problematic at the individual level, we should be skeptical about its efficacy at the collective level as well. The idea that competition is the handmaiden of social progress cannot simply be assumed. Years ago sociologist Rosabeth Moss Kantor sharply challenged the efficiency of the predominant hierarchical/competitive organizational model that typifies corporations. Her investigations revealed much inefficiency, including widespread shirking, and hoarding of information. People in competitive work environments are also nervous, anxious, and resentful.[17]

Competition tends to encourage "lean, mean, corporate machines," but progress can depend upon being "wasteful." In its more halcyon days of corporate dominance for example, IBM would often hire smart people to sit around and think, even if they were not immediately "productive." Or, consider the search for a cure for AIDS, which, if discovered, would certainly qualify as an indicator of social progress. Highly competitive companies, operating on narrow profit margins, could not afford to make investments that would be unlikely to yield a return because failure could mean disaster. Additionally, competitive companies would hoard information in an effort to maximize their advantages over their competitors. Two companies might each have solved a piece of the puzzle, but without sharing information, the puzzle's answer remains a mystery. Thus, efforts in this kind of research area would be greatly inhibited without the intervention of that old monopoly power, the federal government. Our government funds lots of AIDS research that ultimately will prove unproductive. Inevitably it will "waste" money, hoping that some of this research—it is impossible to predict which—will yield the desirable results. The government also then serves as a clearinghouse to publicize the results of research.

A few years ago, Senator William Proxmire attracted favorable publicity by initiating the Golden Fleece Awards. These awards were designed to highlight the supposed idiocy of government bureaucrats willing to fund esoteric research projects. Today, the popular media still enjoy castigating the government for its "wasteful" spending on silly research. Yet the fact is that much of the progress in scientific, technological, and medical research in this century is the result of government willingness to take chances—even to be, by some definition, wasteful.

In the competitive model, competition promotes social progress by eliminating the weak. Competition produces failure, but this is seen as good, like weeding a garden. Yet, despite the widespread acceptance of competition as an abstract social idea, there remains a stubborn unwillingness to accept its logic in much of our everyday life. Failure is cushioned in many ways, through bankruptcy laws that forgive debt, through government unemployment and welfare programs and, for large companies, through corporate bailouts. Thus, in the eighties, the Chrysler Corporation was saved by huge government loans. And the staggering costs resulting from the failure of savings and loan companies after profit-driven risky investment strategies were borne by the government—that is, the rest of us—as well. There was much brave talk about letting such companies accept the consequences of their poor management decisions, but the fact was these consequences were unacceptable. In today's highly interdependent economy, too many would have been hurt too badly to allow such failures to occur. This reality suggests an underlying discomfort with competition that is difficult to confront directly because of its prominence in the culture. Responses to its unpleasant effects are instead jerry-built and ad hoc.

As a ubiquitous cultural characteristic, competition inevitably generates a perspective that also narrows our vision. Thus, capitalism is represented in U.S. society as reflecting the essence of competition. One sharp critic of the ethic of competition believes that it largely has grown out of the system of capitalism.[18] To argue against competition seems to argue against capitalism itself. While it is true that there are inherently competitive features in capitalism, its development also requires extraordinary cooperation. Adam Smith, the founding theorist of capitalism, saw this clearly. The efficiency of capitalism, as Smith represented it in *The Wealth of Nations*, lay in the division of labor. The manufacture of pins, Smith argued in his major illustration, would be much more efficient if workers were singly engaged in the various phases of the manufacturing process. Many have criticized the division of labor for its dehumanizing effects. What is missed in this debate over the division of labor is the extraordinary cooperation required. The levels of cooperation required have grown with each stage of capitalist development, as the economy becomes increasingly interconnected.

Similarly, our culture encourages the imposition of a competitive frame on the world of sports. The much proclaimed value of sport is that it makes us better competitors. What tends to be forgotten is that sport is equally about cooperation. Athletes frequently report that one of the most satisfying aspects of sports for them is seeing talented teammates blend their diverse skills in ways that makes the whole greater than the sum of its parts.[19] The rewards of competition are by nature ephemeral. Last year's winner soon becomes irrelevant in the wake of ever more competition. In contrast, the camaraderie engendered by the cooperative aspects of sport endures, and many athletes note that this is a source of great pleasure.

In a cooperative, problem-solving setting the contributions of everyone are appreciated and rewarded because they are needed. Cooperation directs attention toward what people can do rather than what they cannot. It is also more consonant with the instinct for sociability. Working with others to achieve some end yields great satisfaction. It nurtures both social and ethical bonds precisely because the end is shared. For these reasons it encourages the best efforts of all. One of the interesting research findings in the field of education is that cooperative learning improves the performance of all. Popular wisdom has it that smarter students, for example, should be separated from their slower peers so as not to "hold them back" in their learning. Yet when these students are placed in cooperative groups of students with mixed abilities, everyone benefits—including the smarter students.[20]

To understand why competition remains a core value of U.S. culture, we must consider who benefits from its promotion. One such group is those having things to sell. Competitive flames are fanned because competition stimulates the sale of goods. In our society acquisition has become a major form of competition. This is a subject to which we will return in later chapters.

Additionally, it is obvious that a widely accepted ethic of competition benefits those who are already the most favored in this society. This group benefits in two ways. First, as Andrew Carnegie and his friends recognized more than one hundred years ago, the acceptance of the ethic of competition confers legitimacy on the most successful. If life is seen as a competitive struggle in which some win and some lose, those who are at the top—assuming the game has been fairly played—are then thought to be the most able, the best competitors, and the most deserving. The belief that competition is natural directs attention away from the kind of game being played toward competition itself.

The second benefit enjoyed by this group is that, to the extent that the society actually *is* competitive, they will always be advantaged—often cumulatively so. Public schools enjoy broad legitimacy in this country in part because they are viewed by many as compensating for the inherited disadvantages in the "game of life." Because they are open to all, schools supposedly offer a relatively equal chance for all to succeed. Those who are disadvantaged can, through their own effort and with the help of public education, compete fairly in society. This belief about competition is greatly enhanced by the U.S. cultural characteristic of individualism, which holds that there are no significant social impediments to advancement. The reality is, however, that public schools do not come close to leveling the playing field. Many of the wealthiest citizens bypass the public schools altogether, opting to send their children to more exclusive private schools. In the public school system itself, great inequalities abound, with per pupil expenditures sometimes three times greater in wealthy districts than for poorer areas within the same metropolitan region. Outside of school, the children of the wealthy are conferred additional advantages including tutors, travel, computers, and education camps. Legacies and private contributions increase the likelihood that the children of the wealthy will get into elite colleges, which will confer additional advantages to them.

Competition benefits the status quo in other ways as well. As we have

seen, it promotes social distance and isolation. It works against the solidarity that is the stuff of political movements. It directs attention away
from questions of mutual obligation. Gramsci would see hegemony at work
in America, as competition is a broadly accepted social norm. It satisfies his
hegemonic conditions, described in Chapter One. Competition is a world
view operating for the benefit of the few, promoted by various social institutions such as schools and the mass media, and internalized by those
who are exploited by the concept. Those who benefit from the propagation
of this social norm do not, in fact, take it all that seriously. At a minimum,
a true ethic of competition would require the elimination of inheritance.
Even Andrew Carnegie recognized this truth. Or, considering the other
advantages that the wealthiest citizens enjoy, it would require—not equal
expenditures in public schooling—but spending three or four times more on
the education of children who come from poor families, as Jonathan Kozol
has argued.[21]

Competition is not the unmitigated good it is reputed to be by the
conventional wisdom. It is not natural, certainly not at the levels commonly experienced in U.S. culture. Even if it were natural, it is far from
clear that it should be promoted. It might be a trait that should be mini-
mized. When considered closely, many of the reputed benefits of competition are chimerical. Whatever benefits it may bring to the society must be
weighed against its harmful effects that are sometimes dimly recognized
but rarely fully considered. We shall discuss additional political consequences of competition in Chapter Eight. First, however, we must consider
two other important cultural characteristics.

NOTES

1. Gordon S. Wood, *The Radicalism of the American Revolution,* New York: Vintage, 1993, ch 17.
2. Alfie Kohn, *No Contest,* New York: Houghton Mifflin, 1992.
3. For an excellent account of Social Darwinism see, Richard Hofstadter, *Social
   Darwinism in American Thought,* New York: Beacon Press, 1955.
4. Hofstadter, *op. cit.,* p.31.
5. Prominent opponents of Social Darwinism included Jane Addams's Settle-
   ment House Movement, the Social Gospel movement, and Edward Bellamy's
   Nationalist Movement. See Hofstadter for a useful account of this dissent.
6. Douglas MacArthur's speech at 1949 Army–Navy Football game.
7. Sigmund Freud, *Civilization and its Discontents*, Chicago, IL: University of
   Chicago Press, 1950.
8. See, for example, Michael Argyle, *Cooperation: The Basis of Sociability*, London: Routledge Press, 1991.
9. See Kohn, *op. cit.,* p. 22.

10. Margaret Mead, ed., *Cooperation and Competition Among Primitive Peoples*, Boston, MA: Beacon Press, 1961.

11. Abraham Kaplan, *The Conduct of Inquiry*, San Francisco, CA: Chandler Press, 1964, ch. 10.

12. David W. Johnson, Geoffrey Maruyama, Roger Johnson, Deborah Nelson, and Linda Skon, "Effects of Cooperative, Competitive, and Individualistic Goal Structures on Achievement: A Meta-Analysis," *Psychological Bulletin*, 1981, Vol. 89, No. 1, pp. 47–62.

13. Robert L. Helmrich, Janet T. Spence, William E. Beane, G. William Lucker, and Karen A. Matthews, "Making It in Academic Psychology: Demographic and Personality Correlates of Attainment," *Journal of Personality and Social Psychology*, 1980, Vol. 39, No. 5, pp. 896–908.

14. See Janet T. Spence, ed., *Achievement and Achievement Motives*, San Francisco, CA: W.H. Freeman and Company, 1983, Ch. 1.

15. See Spence, *op. cit.,* pp. 53–61.

16. For a fascinating history of the origins and development of the SAT test, see Nicholas Lemann, *The Big Test: The Secret History of the American Meritocracy*, New York: Farrar, Straus & Giroux, 2000.

17. Rosabeth Moss Kantor, *Men and Women of the Corporation*, New York: Basic Books, 1977.

18. See Kohn, *op. cit.,* pp. 59–78.

19. See, for example, Bill Bradley, *Values of the Game*, New York: Artisan Press, 1998; and Bill Russell, *Second Wind: The Memoirs of an Opinionated Man*, New York: Random House, 1979.

20. Jeannie Oakes, *Keeping Track*, New Haven, CT: Yale University Press, 1985.

21. Jonathan Kozol, *Savage Inequalities*, New York: Crown, 1991.

5

On the Road Again
Mobility and American Life

Few novelists rival Mark Twain in the ability to evoke core features of American culture. Huck Finn, the irresistible scamp in Twain's most famous novel, serves as an outstanding example of this evocation.[1] Bursting with the untamed energy of the frontier, Huck can never quite adapt to Aunt Sally's attempts to make him a "responsible" person. Her fondest desire is to domesticate Huck, to teach him the rules of "sivilized" society, to give him a "place." Huck tries to adapt, but ultimately he cannot. Domestication goes against his nature and proves too restraining, and the novel closes as Huck "lights out for the territories." He is uncertain what lies ahead of him, but this uncertainty is part of the novel's charm. He knows he cannot abide civilization because "I been there before." This taking off is a moment of great exhilaration for Huck, and for Twain as well, whose own life embodied a zest for mobility and adventure.

This attitude, this resistance to stasis, is fundamental to our consciousness. To be American is to be on a search, to be heading somewhere. It is a core characteristic of the culture. Population movement is, of course, as old as human history, and in recent years, socio-political events have sparked huge population movements throughout the world. Since the mid-sixties, the number of refugees in the world has increased more than sevenfold, to fifteen million people today. In less economically developed countries, movement to urban areas has catapulted cities like Calcutta, São Paulo, and Mexico City to the front ranks of the world's most populous cities. The propensity for mobility is universal and must be in part genetic. Mobility requires imagination, the ability to recognize multiple possibilities. Perhaps it grows out of the human capacity for negative thinking that Kenneth Burke identifies in his definition of our species.

It is the argument of this chapter, however, that no modern society rivals ours in the value it places on mobility. For nomadic societies—our only potential rivals in this area—mobility is a quite different phenomenon. Following weather patterns or the migration of life-sustaining herds, a nomadic society moves its entire culture. Like the earth's movement around the sun, nomadic movement is so integral to the culture that it generates little *sense* of mobility. In contrast, the idea of mobility in our culture is radically individualized. To a unique degree, Americans share Huck's consciousness, a recognition that movement involves separation from established patterns of living. The incessant comings and goings of Americans are keenly felt, and contribute to our national character.

It is not simply physical mobility—moving from place to place—that is important to us. Americans also value movement along various social and economic scales. Between the polarities of "being and becoming," Americans are much fonder of the latter. The notions of self-improvement, getting ahead, and making progress are part of the famous American sense of social mobility. Such mobility is inherent in the American Dream. We are reluctant to accept our place on the social scale and, instead, dream of being elsewhere, of progressing, of exceeding the accomplishments of our parents. Although physical and social mobility are analytically distinct, in life experience they may be merged. A move to a better house in the suburbs often reflects the drive for both kinds of mobility. Life is leaving, breaking away, struggling upward. It is Huck, not Aunt Sally, who is the American hero.

Simple geographic fate was undoubtedly critical to the development of mobility as an American cultural value. In part, Americans have moved historically because they could. The term used by Europeans to describe their encounter with the western hemisphere has today devolved into a cliché. The "New World" is now just a term we encounter in history books. We think of it as little different, really, from New Brunswick or New Mexico. The dazzling possibilities that the "New World" suggested to the European consciousness are easily missed in today's smaller and more settled world. As we shall see, Europeans were in fact ambivalent about these possibilities, but certainly for many the new world carried a quite literal meaning. To these, it represented a place where the failures of Europe could be left behind, where one could start over, even where history could begin anew.

Tom Paine, the revolutionary pamphleteer who gained international fame with the publication of *Common Sense* in 1776, captures exactly this sentiment in his essay, *Hymen and Cupid*, published a year earlier. Written as an extended metaphor, this tract was a plea to Americans to bury the European past and to start history anew. Paine captures much of the spirit of Puritan John Winthrop's ringing declaration 150 years earlier, that the task for those arriving in this new world was to create a "shining city on a hill." Eden, Arcadia, Shangri La, had long been poetic and religious fantasies in the European consciousness. The "New World," it seemed, offered a chance for their physical realization. That this land was to be enjoyed after the survival of a perilous ocean voyage, adumbrating the dangerous trek of John Bunyan's fictional Pilgrim to reach heaven, could only reinforce this image.

Much American history can be organized around the theme of population movement. The unprecedented mobility in colonial America has been called "the basic fact of early American history . . . in which people moved as never before—from village to village, from colony to colony, over distances of ten, a hundred, even a thousand miles."[2] Physical mobility has remained a continuing fact of American life. This contrasts with other countries' histories over the same period. In Asia, Europe, Africa, and the Middle East, there have been dramatic and frequent changes in geopolitical boundaries over the last three hundred years, as there have been in the United States. What is distinctive about U.S. history is that these changes have also been accompanied by huge migratory shifts. For three centuries, American migratory patterns were largely westward, as European immigrants and their progeny pushed toward the Pacific Ocean and their "manifest destiny," subduing or eradicating indigenous cultures. The movement west has never stopped, and California now has more than twelve percent of the nation's population. In the last 150 years, however, other notable migratory patterns have occurred as well. Industrialization and two world wars left their imprint on national mobility patterns, pulling people to the north. In recent decades, the post–industrial society has witnessed extensive movement to the south.

Overlaying such broad regional patterns of migration is the movement of people from rural to urban environments. Census Bureau reports show that the United States first became a predominantly urban society in 1920. The fact that for the great bulk of our history more people lived in rural areas than in urban centers indicates the spaciousness of this land. The population of cities swelled during the Industrial Revolution, then burst into suburbs. By 1960, just 40 years after we became a predominantly urban nation, more people lived in suburbs than in cities. Geographic movement remains unabated. Suburbs now fade into more distant urban zones demographers classify as "exurban." Urbanologists chart the course of suburban sprawl and muse about its consequences.[3]

This inclination to move has been variously noted and celebrated throughout our history. In 1831 Tocqueville wrote of citizens of this young nation, "Once they migrate, they circulate."[4] Mark Twain's romanticism was paralleled by Walt Whitman's "Song of the Open Road," and Horace Greeley soberly advised the young men of his generation to "go west." A hundred years later, Jack Kerouac, guru to the beatnik counterculture, titled his autobiographical novel *On the Road*.

The Census Bureau reports that in recent decades between 16 and 20 percent of our population has moved *each year*, more than double the rate of any European nation. Some of this movement is of course driven by poverty, as the poor are forced to make way for various forms of development, including highways, athletic stadiums, and gentrification. This in itself offers oblique testimony of the integration of mobility into our consciousness: Moving people, even against their will, simply is not that big a deal and may even be regarded as a sign of progress. It is also evident, however, that most movement is voluntary. Images of utopia, perhaps a bit faded, still motivate us. Americans continue to move to the golden state, or north to Alaska, to the sun belt, to an urban center, or to a suburban "gated community" with images of utopia on their minds.

Upward mobility animates the intergenerational stories Americans share. Oral histories chronicle sagas of physical and social mobility. The universality of this theme is illustrated by Alex Haley's extremely popular TV miniseries, *Roots*, which in 1977 drew huge audiences from all racial groups. The program's popularity was somewhat surprising because, for the standards of network television at that time, it was unusually frank about slavery. Some felt this would reduce white viewership. Yet white viewers had no trouble recognizing *Roots* as a quintessential American saga. Despite its title, it was less about roots than it was a story of people in the direst of circumstances struggling upward toward a life of respectability—an updating and colorization of Horatio Alger.

Since physical mobility is integral to the American experience, it is not surprising that social mobility is prevalent as well. The idea of getting ahead has long been identified with the idea of getting on. Professor Wood notes that shortly after the revolution a truly radical idea—the idea of the self-made man—took hold in America. In the eighteenth-century western world, even in colonial America, social mobility was not celebrated because social location was seen as a reflection of the fundamentally different natures of the classes. Thus, the poor were poor because of who they were. Typically a man who had risen to social prominence would try to hide his humble origins, as they suggested a violation of the natural order. Ben Franklin's *Autobiography* was unusual in its celebration of humble origins. But Franklin's autobiography was published posthumously, and at his funeral in 1790, his eulogist passed over his early life as being too embarrassing to dwell upon.

As the nineteenth century dawned, however, Americans began to celebrate the idea of the self-made man, and even to be somewhat disdainful of inherited wealth. This shocking turn of events was possible only in America, and the physical mobility of the population was an important reason why. In a society where people were moving constantly, where new communities were being formed daily, traditional hierarchies were undermined. There could be no "prominent families" in new communities. Many have noted that this condition of unusual equality was a great stimulus to democracy in America. It also contributed to a growing sense that anyone could "make it" in the new world.

THE MACHINE IN THE GARDEN

Mobility is connected to a conflict that Leo Marx sees at the root of American culture.[5] This is the conflict between the natural and the created world, between action and stasis, between our simultaneous desires to live in harmony with nature and to change it. The conflict was distinctly American because early European settlers were confronted with both possibilities so vividly. Despite some inconvenient indigenous cultures, America seemed like raw nature itself to many Europeans. Thus, an actual encounter with Eden, previously the stuff of dreams, seemed like a real possibility. Additionally, this encounter occurred at the onset of the Industrial Revolution in Europe, precisely the time when the possibilities of transforming and exploiting nature were beginning to explode.

Professor Marx called one attempted reconciliation of this conflict the "middle landscape," and he uses the garden as a metaphor to represent it. A garden seems to reconcile nature and development. The garden's affinity with the natural world is apparent; it is in many ways a tribute to it. The garden represents order, harmony, control. But the garden is *transformed* nature. It is humanity's improvement on nature, our way, with devices of our own creation (symbolized by the machine), of correcting God. The problem Marx identifies is that no one has been able to specify the right balance between the machine and the garden. Because the middle landscape papered over the conflict, there was no reason to restrain the "progress" introduced by the machine, and so the quest became endless and destructive—a constant movement toward "something else." Thus the machine triumphed in the New World—as it had in the old—but not without cost, and Marx argues that "It remained for our serious writers to discover the meaning inherent in the contradiction."[6]

A major tributary of the American literary stream arises from this conflict. In several great American novels, the symbol of advancing technology is the very machinery of mobility, and it is always destructive. A steamship overturns the idyllic raft of Huck and Jim as they are in reverie and repose on the Mississippi; the *Pequod* carries Ahab and his crew to their doom in the pursuit of Moby Dick; Gatsby's fabulous cream-colored car, which symbolizes his high lifestyle, becomes the source of his undoing. Sister Carrie begins her spiritual and physical journey on a train to Chicago and escapes via train with Hurstwood to New York to begin a new life. Hurstwood's final undoing comes as a lowly trolley driver in the streets of New York, and the novel ends with Carrie in a rocking chair—moving, but going nowhere.

Other famous works of American literature, while not necessarily conforming to Marx's paradigm, also wrestle with the notion of restlessness, mobility, and quest. The idea of rising and falling in society is a central motif in American literature, as writers from a wide variety of perspectives muse about this American phenomenon. William Dean Howells's *The Rise of Silas Lapham*, published in 1885, is an early example of this genre. In the opening pages of this novel, Silas Lapham takes great pride driving his fine trotter through the streets of Boston, leaving a hundred "rival sledges" in his wake. This incident serves as a metaphor for the hero's spectacular rise from impoverished rural Vermont to the upper reaches of Boston society. This rise, however, is fraught with consequences, as Lapham loses his moral moorings. Lapham's social mobility had been achieved by an indifference toward others. At a dinner party that is the crucial scene of the novel, Lapham comes to realize the emptiness of his life. His new found moral sense is accompanied by his economic ruin. Some reviewers of the day were puzzled by the title of the novel, but of course Howells believed that Lapham truly rose when he rejected social mobility.[7] The (at least) ambiguous consequences of social mobility resonate in such prominent works as *The Bell Jar*, *Catcher in the Rye*, *The Death of a Salesman*, *The Autobiography of Miss Jane Pittman*, and John Updike's Rabbit trilogy. Other novels explicitly use physical mobility as a metaphor for social mobility.[8] Clearly, it is an important theme in American literature.

MOBILITY AND POPULAR CULTURE

Mobility has also been reflected in popular culture as well, albeit often without the critical edge evident in the more "serious" American literature. Rather, mobility tends to be accepted as a simple fact of life, and its virtues more readily accented. One study of juvenile fiction between 1900 and 1940, for example, indicates that the automobile played a central role to the story lines.[9] The car simultaneously symbolized prowess and control, technical proficiency, adventure, and freedom. The potential of the automobile for capturing the imagination of the young was recognized very early. The first number of the twenty-two volume *Motor Boys* series appeared in 1906. It was followed shortly by a popular *Motor Girls* series.

The protagonist in the popular *Tom Swift* series, which ran from 1910 to 1935, is a mechanical genius preoccupied with the potential of air travel. The automobile is also an important feature of both the *Hardy Boys* and the *Nancy Drew* series. Such works highlighted a world in which ". . . youthful characters could compete with adults on an equal basis; [automobiles] offered mobility, speed, protection, and often the opportunity to demonstrate exceptional physical coordination."[10]

As the twentieth century began, the automobile was quickly romanticized and became a major subject in popular music. The dominant theme in this music is the liberating potential of the car. It offered literal flight from reigning social norms, which made it attractive, if ambivalently so. Many popular car songs of the day had frankly sexual overtones. One study identifies more than 120 songs released between 1905 and 1907 that identified the car with an increased potential for sexual conquest, including the infamous, "I'd Rather Go Walking with the Man I Love Than Ride in Your Car (You Cad)."[11] Cars were thus viewed as means of escape, in these instances from overly intrusive social norms or the prying eyes of family.

Songs romanticizing the railroad and the highway are fundamental in both the folk and the blues traditions. Generations of bluegrass fiddlers have mimicked the beckoning wail of the "Orange Blossom Special," or eulogized "The Wreck of the '97," even as their blues brethren have been "goin' down the road feelin' bad." Country and Western music has probably given even more attention to the road and to the fluidity of life. In the days of radio dominance, Bill Mack broadcast his legendary all night, trucker-oriented "Open Road" show from a 50,000 watt AM station in Texas, sending personal messages, road condition information, as well as country music across the nation. Today, no self-respecting C & W artist is without his or her panoply of road songs. These range from the joyful "On the Road Again," through the desperate "White Line Fever," to the plaintive, "Leave Me Tomorrow (You've Hurt Me Enough for Today)."

Growing out of the blues, folk, and country traditions, rock and roll also uses mobility as a central motif. Leading authority Sam Phillips— the man who launched the careers of Elvis Presley, Jerry Lee Lewis, and Chuck Berry—pinpoints the beginning of Rock and Roll with the 1951 release of "Rocket 88" by Jackie Brentson and the Kings of Rhythm.[12] This song, in which Brentson beckons the female listener to go riding with him in his flashy new car, soon became number one on rhythm-and-blues charts. The car has been a staple in rock and roll ever since. Elvis was devoted to the car, both in song and in his personal life. His Graceland Mansion in Memphis is awash in Presley automobiles. Chuck Berry, Buddy Holly, the Beach Boys, Jan and Dean, the Cars, Bruce Springsteen, Tracy Chapman, Phish, and countless others tell us that adventure, good times, sexual fulfillment, danger, and death—in short, all of life's real possibilities—are out there, on the road.

Since mobility implies restlessness and dissatisfaction, this cultural characteristic can appeal to those who are socially alienated. Hence the drifter, the antihero who seems to move aimlessly from place to place, is also a cultural icon. The aimlessness suggests a reluctance to accept dominant social norms, but on the other hand movement is itself a norm. The young Brando, embodying working-class alienation in the fifties, restlessly roams the countryside on a motorcycle in the movie "The Wild Ones" and is still imitated by millions. The Solomon R. Guggenheim Museum in New York has a well-deserved reputation for attractive and innovative special exhibits. Their 1998 exhibit "The Art of the Motorcycle" proved popular even by that museum's lofty standards. Over a three-month period, the 111 motorcycles on display drew more than 300,000 patrons, the highest attendance of any exhibit in the museum's history.

The Beat Poets of the fifties represented a perhaps more cerebral kind of rebellion. With their emphasis on fluid social relations and being "on the road," however, they were less counter-cultural than they imagined. A decade later the spiritual heirs to the Beats, the hippies, also found mobility to be an appealing lifestyle, as they trekked across country in colorful VW microbuses adorned with the admonitory bumper sticker "Keep on Trucking." Following the Grateful Dead from city to city was considered by many to be the very essence of right living. A drug experience was called "tripping." Several classic films of that era, including "Bonnie and Clyde," "The Graduate," and "Easy Rider," are each in their own way odes to mobility. Working class gangs like the Hell's Angels and the Outlaws express their rebellion in mobility and vie for road space in rural areas with the elderly, sedate drivers of airstream trailers, who have themselves "retired" to an ideal life of permanent mobility.

In such a cultural environment, it is not surprising that movement emerges as a national requirement. We are constantly positing new frontiers to conquer. Whether outward, upward, or inward, the point is to be on a journey. Our language is infused with metaphors invoking this ideal. At work, an effective employee is described as a "person on the move," or "a mover and a shaker." During times of felt ineffectiveness, we may describe ourselves as being "on a treadmill," suggesting the ultimate frustration: motion without mobility. A difficult problem invokes the fear of being "stuck." Young people are constantly counselled to "keep on track." A powerful political speech is described as "moving." In moments of intimacy we tell our lovers, "you move me," or perhaps we ask whether "the earth moved." "How's it going?" we regularly ask acquaintances when we greet them. When we feel good we are "up"; when we despair, we are "down." Either way we are in motion—heading somewhere.

The value of mobility is reinforced in the modern American workplace. The idea of a "career ladder" has always been integral to industrial society, even if the ladder proved to be far shorter than the ideal suggested.

In post–industrial society, mobility has taken a new form. While earlier capitalism was typified by routinized work that gave little in the way of emotional return, at least it was a constant out of which one could construct a sensible linear narrative for one's life. One could say, "This is what I do, this is why I do it, this is where I'm going." At least one knew who one's enemies were. Richard Sennett[13] has chronicled the emergence of a "new capitalism" in which mobility is so ubiquitous that even these former certainties are called into question. The idea of a career is in retreat. Mobility is king, but it is not structured mobility, the mobility of a ladder. Rather, it is anomic mobility.

Today, workers with at least two years of college can expect eleven job changes in their adult work lives. In this newer system of perpetual downsizings, mergers, temporary work, and international relocations, there are fewer fixed rules to rely on. "No long term" is increasingly the reality. The modern diffusion of responsibility (but not control) has made it difficult even to identify the source of this new reality. "Change" just happens, a concatenation of causeless events. In such a world, where instability and movement are the dominant norms, constructing a narrative of identity becomes problematic. "The psyche dwells in a state of endless becoming—a self which is never finished."[14] Indeed, the idea of mobility is so paramount, it is difficult for those who oppose such trends to muster a vocabulary of opposition.

The pervasive wanderlust that infuses the culture is subject to diverse interpretations. On the one hand, it suggests a spirit of adventure and optimism. The courage of our forebears in taking a perilous ocean voyage, or struggling great distances through hostile terrain, is widely recognized and lauded. The "promised land" imagery of America, now centuries old, remains strong even for recent immigrants. Furthermore, non-nomadic social movement implies optimism. When people move, it is usually out of a sense that things can be better.

On the other hand, a constant impulse toward mobility can be disquieting. It may reflect feelings of inadequacy and an inability to cope with current circumstances. The more familiar imagery we connect to mobility is that of "striving toward" or "reaching out," but it can also represent a frenetic "fleeing from," an uncertainty about the self, a compulsive incapacity for contentment. Although less promoted, this image is also familiar, and it has been a central theme in American letters.

THE CAR

Outside of national defense, government spending is not broadly popular in the United States. As we have seen, this relative stinginess accords with our cultural traditions. Hence it is interesting that on June 9, 1998, President Clinton signed a six-year $218 billion Highway Bill, formally known as the Transportation Equity Act for the twenty-first century.[15] It was aimed primarily at improving the nation's aging highway system, although it had some funds for mass transit as well. It enjoyed bipartisan support, easily passing both houses of the Republican-controlled Congress. This huge bill was full of the kind of pork barrel projects politicians find irresistible. For example, it provided $640 million for transportation assistance to cities hosting Olympic events, and it earmarked $50 million for ferry construction in Alaska. And of course the bill had strong support from the construction industry.

More than anything else, however, the bill reflects our longstanding commitment to the automobile as a means of transportation. This commitment has grown steadily throughout this century, with perhaps the definitive watershed being the passing of the National Highway Act in 1956. Under the leadership of President Dwight Eisenhower, this Act authorized federal support for the construction of our interstate highway system, easily the most expensive public works project in the history of the nation.[16]

The importance of automobiles is revealed in many ways. Except for a home, they are likely to be the most expensive things Americans buy, and they are purchased many times throughout one's lifetime. In 1992, the most recent year for which data are available, we spent over $600 billion for cars, parts, gas, insurance, licenses, and tolls. In contrast we spent $5.7 billion to ride rapid transit, and $369 billion on groceries in that year.[17] Additionally, there are the huge indirect costs of highway and parking lot construction and maintenance. Highway patrols and traffic courts further increase the price tag for the car.

Things other than cost also suggest the significance of automobility to Americans. Car magazines proliferate. People wait for the annual fall display of new vehicle models with eager anticipation and flock to auto shows throughout the country. In Chicago, the Auto Show is held at McCormack Place, the largest exhibition center in the United States. It regularly draws more than one million people, ten times the audience of any other exhibit held at that facility. Many spend countless hours working on their cars—souping up the engines or customizing the interior or the body. Various kinds of car clubs draw people together. Acquiring a driver's license is a major rite of passage. The gift of a car frequently symbolizes the occurrence of a major life event, such as high school graduation or an important anniversary. As nowhere else, Americans love automobility.

Some believe this devotion to the automobile is the result of a conspiracy of car manufacturers and oil companies to suppress alternative forms of transportation. While these interests have never been reluctant to exercise their considerable political clout in pursuit of profits, there is another important dimension to the story: This political power has always been exercised in a very congenial cultural context. Of all the forms of population movement, it is the car that best allows for the expression of the cultural value of mobility. No other form of transportation provides as much opportunity to "light out for the territories." If the cowboy, loping over the range in search of freedom and adventure, remains a central mythic figure, the car is the logical heir to the horse. John Wayne would not ride rapid transit. The historic devotion to mobility made the car a very easy sell in America. Since the days of Henry Ford, Americans have been fiercely attached to automobiles. Between 1929 and 1939, as this nation suffered the greatest economic depression in its history—more than a quarter of the work force was unemployed—automobile ownership *increased* by three million. Hard times did not stop the purchase of automobiles. It is instructive that in Steinbeck's classic novel depicting the suffering of this era, the Joads, though they were dirt-poor dust bowl refugees, had a vehicle that took them to California and the Grapes of Wrath.

David Rieff's meditation on the meaning of modern day Los Angeles directly connects American affection for the car with our historic quest for mobility.[18] He is led to his musings while encountering virtual gridlock on the Los Angeles interstate system. How is it, he wonders, that so many individuals can sit for so long in their cars? He believes the answer is because cars symbolize "breaking free" to Americans. Americans, he argues, continue to cast their biographies as one long drama of breaking free— what we have identified as mobility. For Rieff, Americans see life as a series of escapes: from family; from home towns; from inherited beliefs; and, these days, from marriage. Rieff views the car as the ultimate expression of the decontextualized self.

The connections of the automobile to physical mobility are obvious, but, from its inception, it has served as an important embodiment of social mobility as well. The initial purchase of a car moves us up the social hierarchy, and further bench marks are established as one moves from a Tempo, to a Buick, to a Lexus. Historian Clay McShane's study of the national transition to automobility reveals the powerful role status played in this transition.[19] His systematic assessment of all the references to cars carried in *The New York Times* during the year of 1908 reveals their historic significance as status symbols. Most of the information about cars in 1908 was carried on the society pages, where the motor escapades of socially prominent people were duly noted.

Status consciousness with respect to the automobile can be seen in other ways as well. In the early decades of the twentieth century, many white Americans greatly resented black Americans who had the temerity to purchase and drive their own autos. Such ownership was often taken by whites as a sign that blacks were getting "uppity" and hence threatening the social status of whites. In the South, black drivers were often run off the road by offended white drivers. In a highly promoted match race, famous race car driver Barney Oldfield defeated Jack Johnson, the menacing African-American boxing champion who also dabbled in racing. The next day the headline in the *New York Sun* read: "White Race Saved!" Vestiges of this sensibility remain even today, as one frequently hears references to "welfare queens driving Cadillacs." Black citizens, who are cited for traffic violations far more frequently than whites, are familiar with a special category of wrongdoing: DWB—driving while black.

McShane views the appeal of automobility in part as an antidote to the increasing sense of male emasculation that accompanied industrialization. Cars were actively promoted as a means to recover one's manhood. Automobility (ownership, operation, and maintenance) was marketed as a male province. In a revealing sign of the times, many considered women to be genetically incapable of automobility. They supposedly lacked the dexterity, strength, and mechanical sensibilities necessary for operating automobiles. To contradict this common view, suffragettes would often drive automobiles in parades promoting their right to vote. This pointedly illustrated their inherent social equality and was considered a provocative act by many men.

THE SOCIAL COSTS OF AUTOMOBILITY

Every modern society must face the problems of transporting goods and people. While the automobile is of course internationally significant, no other nation matches ours in its relentless devotion to this particular solution to mobility. So ubiquitous is the car that it is tempting to see it, not as one policy option, but as part of the natural order of things, the consequence of some meta-logic with regard to social movement. Americans are well versed in the advantages of automobility. These are so obvious that alternative policy options for population movement seem almost subversive. It is useful, therefore, to consider briefly some of the costs of automobility.[20]

As we have noted, cars are enormously expensive to own, operate, insure, and maintain. While they are efficient in transporting individuals, socially, cars are an efficiency disaster. As ownership grows, more land is given over to concrete—for wider, more elaborate highways and for parking. Highway analysts reveal that, because parking facilities must be designed for periods of maximum use, each vehicle in operation requires six parking spaces. Parking space around a shopping mall or a football stadium—unused most of the time—is necessary to accommodate the demand during peak times.

Studies show that new highway construction does little to decrease congestion; it simply increases the number of cars being used. As a consequence, today Americans spend more time in their cars than they ever have. As car usage grows, other transportation options are crowded out, thus discriminating against those who cannot drive, including the young, many elderly, as well as physically-challenged people. As a consequence, those who can drive face increasing demands to drive those who cannot. Partly in response to this, in many families today, the number of cars is equivalent to the number of people eligible to drive in that family. Three- and four-car families do not think of themselves as extravagant. Rather they are simply adapting to today's autocentric society.

Cars pose serious ecological and health problems as well. They are a significant drain on finite natural resources. Heavy salting of streets in northern cities during winter threaten water supplies. Highly toxic auto emissions generate disease and are a major source of ozone depletion. Automobility is also the most dangerous form of population movement. Each year more than 40,000 Americans die in auto accidents, and several hundred thousand are injured. Extensive auto usage makes us dependent upon foreign oil that is often controlled by antidemocratic and repressive political regimes. We defend such regimes because we believe it is in "our vital national interests" to do so.

This list is not exhaustive, but it does illustrate the more important, direct social costs of automobility. Beyond these direct costs, the automobile promotes a lifestyle that also has important social implications. The evolution of the vast highway system necessary to support our love for automobility, for example, has had profound effects on social dynamics— a fact noted by numerous social critics.[21] Historically, streets were public meeting places—centers of play, commerce, and public discourse. Streets were, in short, the generators of community. Merchants would ply their wares from carts parked in the streets, neighbors would meet and linger while strolling through them, or beckon from porches. Streets were playgrounds for children. Baseball players like Willie Mays and Joe DiMaggio grew up playing stickball in the streets of New York and San Francisco. Because streets had such general utility, when the early twentieth-century "Better Roads" movement sought to transform streets into more efficient systems of mobility it was met with active resistance, and even violence.

The development of highways was premised upon the idea, now commonplace but once controversial, that mobility is the point of roads. The other functions of roads receded and eventually disappeared. Today, roads are important because they place people in motion. Houston serves as an archetype of what has happened in many newer cities.[22] Beginning in the forties, it succumbed to the imperatives of the automobile and instituted a new highway system that completely restructured the central city. More land in Houston is now given to paved surfaces than to buildings or to green space. The dominance of the highway has eroded the social fabric. Downtown Houston no longer exists as a meaningful social center. Its relevance today is as a transportation grid.

The vestiges of these differing perspectives on the road can still be seen by contrasting older urban neighborhoods with newer suburbs. Older urban centers, largely in place before the automobile came to dominate social movement, are far less accommodating to it. The streets are narrower in the older neighborhoods, and garages, if they are to be found at all, are located off alleys in the back of residential properties. Large front porches, edging residents toward the streets, are typical. Surely it is not an accident that in America's oldest great city, New York, one sees remnants of the battle for the streets, in which pedestrians stubbornly wage a rear guard action.

In the age of automobility, public discourse is also diminished by the fact that increasing portions of everyday life are undertaken from the front seat of a car. Entrepreneurs first hit upon drive-in restaurants and movie theaters. Now people can buy groceries, bank, drop off laundry, attend church, visit funeral parlors, have cars washed, and do other things as well, without leaving their automobiles. This highly individualized convenience comes at the cost of everyday social discourse that is vital to civil society. It erodes some of the mediating institutions that Tocqueville believed were crucial to keep individualism from sliding into egoism.

The social–intercourse–from–the–front–seat–of–the–car phenomenon is not the only thing in the autocentric society that builds a sense of isolation. In the early days of automobility, low powered, open cars traveling on relatively primitive roads that followed the contours of the landscape provided some social connection. Early drives through Central Park in New York were not too different from strolls down Fifth Avenue. Such auto-inspired connection is a thing of the past. Now interstates cut huge concrete swaths through urban spaces, simultaneously obliterating neighborhoods and obscuring what remains. The vast interstate system in Los Angeles, for example, is disconnected from its environs. At any point in this system, one could be anywhere. Only the uniform highway signs provide orientation. There is no sense of Watts on the Harbor Freeway, of East Los Angeles on the San Gabriel Freeway, or of Hollywood on the Hollywood Freeway. On this system, one of the most diverse metropolises in the world seems completely uniform.

Drivers are increasingly disconnected from each other as well. Cars are now enclosed and move at high speeds. The noise generated by high-powered trucks forces windows to be closed, as do air conditioning and stereo systems. These closed windows are often tinted, further discouraging human contact.

In the first decades of automobility, cars invoked freedom. "Come along with me Lucille, in my merry Oldsmobile" reflected the way people tended to think about their cars. Family Sunday drives—moving, but without particular destination—were commonplace and embodied this sense of freedom. This kind of freedom—freedom as individual disconnection—

is not without cost. Today, it can be argued that cars have difficulty even delivering on freedom of this sort. They clog our highways and we can't escape. Commuting time increases, and cars designed to be driven at 75 miles per hour inch along in stop-and-go traffic. In a kind of devil's logic, the more space we give to highway construction, the more congestion and commuting time we endure. Except for teenagers, a car is now the last place one wants to be on a Sunday.

THE AUTOMOBILE AND SUBURBIA

In addition to being a means of physical movement, the car is also an expression of social mobility. Cars convey social status and, perhaps more important, they convey us *to* social status. They have allowed for the universalization of suburbia. Careful studies of social order and land use clearly reveal that the movement to suburbia, and from there to pricier suburbs, is a key indicator of social mobility and status.[23] Suburbs were common before the car was invented, but the car eliminated the necessity of locating suburbs along convenient railroad spurs and was therefore a huge stimulus to suburban proliferation.

Being more dependent on the car, the suburbs pay greater homage to it. Interesting architectural changes in housing have accompanied suburban development.[24] The garage is increasingly prominent and has moved from the back of the property to its front. In many cases the garage dominates the entire structure. They have grown larger and now accommodate two or three cars. From spacious streets motorists can now turn into large driveways leading directly into their automatically-opening garages. The internal entrances of these garages serve as the major points of egress into the house. No longer serving a function, the front porch has shrunk dramatically, or has disappeared entirely. Instead, a sheltered and private patio at the back of the home provides residents with their major access to the outdoors. Today, Huck would have a more difficult time lighting out for the territories, but private retreats abound. They proliferate along the ever-lengthening concrete ribbons that now envelop "the territories."

Some urban historians have seen primal cultural impulses in the development of suburbia.[25] It has been previously noted that the American Dream is intensely private. The private home now rests at its center. In rural and early capitalist America, home and worklife were fused, their boundaries diffuse and overlapping. With the Industrial Revolution, the break between private and public life became sharper. People left their homes to engage in work over which they often had little control. In these circumstances the home became a refuge from the workplace, a "haven in a heartless world." The antisocial quality of the American Dream intensified. The early TV sitcom, *The Honeymooners*, captures this sense precisely as Ralph, the abused and emasculated bus driver, frequently asserted, "A man's home is his castle!" In medieval times, however, the castle had multiple functions. It was a source of protection, but it was also the center of community life. Ralph's castle is simply a fortress against the social forces that buffet and demean him.

As urban life grew more complex in the nineteenth century, it affected not only traditional working-class types like Ralph, but also the ruling elites. Cities swelled and grew more chaotic; streets began to fill with immigrants speaking a variety of languages. Many socially prominent citizens began to feel the cities were spinning out of their control, and they sought refuge in what has been called the "bourgeois utopias" of suburban development.[26] Suburbs reasserted control over the environment and renewed the self-confidence of these elites. There was a religious component to the development of suburbia as well. Catharine Beecher, of the famous evangelical Beecher family, wrote *Treatise on Domestic Economy*, the definitive statement on nineteenth-century American domestic ideology. For Beecher, the home was the best source of Christian morality, and the best homes were separated from the profane concerns of the city.

Today, the American Dream has morphed into the acquisition of a "dream house." "For the first time in history," Delores Hayden has observed, "a civilization created a utopian ideal based on the house rather than on the city or the nation."[27] Since the days of their earliest development in the nineteenth century, homes in suburbia have been marketed as privatized embodiments of the good life. The names of subdivisions in suburban Naperville, Illinois illustrate the general tendency: Rivermist, Winding Creek Estates, Maplebrook, River Oaks, High Meadow, Hunter Wood. Characteristically, suburbs are bucolic compromises. Yards and gardens— the hint of Eden—are an important part of suburban homes. These homes must also be convenient however, and here the automobile came to play a vital role.

This pursuit of personalized Edens has had an ironic effect, as everything beyond one's property lines grows increasingly problematic. T. Coraghessan Boyle effectively captures one sense of this in his novel, *The Tortilla Curtain*. Set in contemporary southern California, the novel's protagonists, a young couple, wish to avoid facing a new social reality—the rising tide of Mexican illegals in their area. Of course their community is highly dependent upon the illegals for gardening, construction, domestic service, and the like. While anxious to make use of these services—they are a great economic blessing—the community steadfastly resists considering their larger meaning. They cannot recognize the humanity of the newcomers, or their connections to them. Instead, they employ guards and build walls around their subdivisions to avoid unwanted contact and social complexity.

At another level, demographers have chronicled the rise of urban sprawl, which one recent report calls "the dark side" of the American

Dream.[28] The consequences of this unplanned, rapid growth are much in evidence: increased traffic congestion, longer commutes, increased dependence on fossil fuels, worsening air and water pollution, lost open space and wetlands, increased flooding, diminished wildlife habitat, and dying city centers. In Atlanta, for example, urban land area increased by 20 percent between 1980 and 1990, and by 47 percent between 1990 and 1996. Green space is being gobbled up by sprawl faster than ever. Every week 500 acres of forest or farm land are plowed under to build parking lots, shopping malls, and housing subdivisions. Motorists in Atlanta now lead the nation in miles driven per person per day. Air pollution has dramatically increased, and the local government is under constant pressure to expand the road system. Thinking privately, as our culture encourages us to, each small decision creating this state of affairs might have made sense. Outside of one's own backyard, however, it is hard to imagine being pleased with what has generally happened to metropolitan Atlanta.

MOBILITY AND POLITICS

Kenneth Burke's definition of human beings recognizes two inherent characteristics that may work at cross purposes. On one hand, humans love order and predictability; on the other we are tinkerers, restless pursuers of change. A social order negating either would be unbearable. A society totally committed to stability would be cruel and oppressive, even antihuman. A society that values only process and flux would also be fundamentally flawed, for it would not provide the mooring that is essential to living. What we need is somehow to balance the contrasting values of being and becoming.

The cultural value of mobility elevates process, becoming, separateness, and in so doing it may obscure the importance of connection and place. In consequence, it may undermine politics, because politics grows out of a recognition of shared fates and common space. Areas with high rates of mobility generate little political activity. This cannot merely be explained by voting residency requirements. While there are solitary actors in politics, politics is more commonly an expression of solidarity. Since it also unifies the past with some vision of the future, some knowledge is important to politics. A person who has just moved into an apartment complex, for example, is likely not to know very much about the history of this new community, and since the new resident probably sees this arrangement as temporary, there is little incentive to unite with others in the complex to achieve some community betterment. In such a fluid situation, there is even a psychological penalty to community attachment. Making friends and getting involved in the community only increases the pain when it is time to move on.

A recent sociological study of 300 neighborhoods found that the quality of relations between neighbors was an important factor in producing safety and security. Calling high quality relations "collective efficacy," the study observed its effects by controlling for other things such as income and ethnicity. Where collective efficacy was high, rates of crime and violence were low. Because of its importance, the researchers were interested in the things that affected collective efficacy. They found one of the key variables was population mobility. The higher the rate of population movement in neighborhoods, the lower the sense of collective efficacy.[29]

The high rates of mobility in colonial America had the effect of diminishing social ties in the colonies. Today, our reverence for mobility has stimulated the rise of quick-response, drive-thru establishments that also undercut community. Everywhere, the emphasis is on speed, on process, on getting on with one's life. A few years ago, the South was notable for its resistance to these forces of modernity. People would linger in stores, inquiring after families and each other. No longer. Now the South has joined the rest of the nation, its citizens wolfing down meals at McDonald's and rushing through lines at Target on their way to—somewhere.

American suburbia, increasingly the "place" of modern life, is not a particularly effective generator of community. Often suburbs are merely way stations on an increasingly dominant transportation grid. They grow out from interstate exchanges, this community on one side of the interchange, that community on the other side. The primary function of many suburban housing tracts is not to stimulate activity, political or otherwise, but to provide respite from an increasingly frenetic world. Radburn, New Jersey, established outside New York City in 1927, became a prototype for much subsequent suburban development.[30] In its early days, it was called "the town for the Motor Age." Dominated by cul-de-sacs, with houses facing away from the street, it encouraged, not community, but solitude.

In his study of Los Angeles, David Rieff ponders the fact that Southern Californians spend an estimated 1.2 billion hours per year idling in their cars and waste 750 million gallons of gasoline doing so. He concludes:[31]

> All the fabled California cults . . . were really far less radical, when you stopped to think about it, than one ordinary resident of the Los Angeles basin, driving alone on the freeway, unencumbered by spouse, children, or relations, through spaces that, unless he has lived or worked there, are more like empty spaces than real places to him. All around him are other, similarly occupied people. . . . [N]obody could have imagined that it would have been possible to so completely decontextualize people, or that the internal combustion engine would have made this atomization seem like a gift.

Steve Martin, himself a product of Southern California suburbia, brilliantly satirizes this decontextualization in his film, *L.A. Story*. As Martin's character and his wife drive down a highway in L.A., on their way to a hurried café latte, double skim-milk, he suddenly realizes it is the first day of spring. He immediately pulls out a hand gun, lowers the car window, and fires randomly at passing motorists, who return his fire. His conversation with his wife, built exclusively around private wants and desires, is uninterrupted.

NOTES

1. Garry Wills uses Huckleberry Finn as a cultural prism through which to understand Ronald Reagan in his book, *Reagan's America*, New York: Penguin, 1987.
2. Gordon S. Wood, *The Radicalism of the American Revolution*, New York: Vintage, 1991, pp. 125–126.
3. Sierra Club Report, *The Dark Side of the American Dream*, Sierra Club, San Francisco, CA, 1998.
4. Cited in Tom Lewis, *Divided Highways*, New York: Viking, 1997, p. 122.
5. Leo Marx, *The Machine in the Garden*, London: Oxford University Press, 1978.
6. Marx, *op. cit.,* p. 226.
7. See Everett Carter, *Howells and the Age of Realism*, Philadelphia, PA: J.B. Lippencott, 1954, pp. 157–169.
8. Prominent examples include *The Great Gatsby, Babbitt, Main Street, The Grapes of Wrath*, and *Zen and the Art of Motorcycle Maintenance*.
9. David K. Vaughan, "Automobile and American Juvenile Series Fiction, 1900–1940," in Jan Jennings, ed., *Roadside America*, Iowa State University Press, 1990.
10. Vaughan, *op. cit.,* p. 78.
11. E.L. Widmer, "Crossroads: The Automobile, Rock and Roll, and Democracy," in Jennings, *op. cit.*
12. Widmer, *op. cit.,* p. 86.
13. Richard Sennett, *The Corrosion of Character*, New York: W.W. Norton, 1998.
14. Sennett, *op. cit.,* p. 133.
15. A summary of the act can be found in Alan K. Ota, "What the Highway Bill Does," *Congressional Quarterly Weekly*, July 11, 1998, pp. 1892–1898.
16. See Tom Lewis, *Divided Highways*, New York: Viking, 1997.
17. Anne Mackin, "The Driven Society: Why Americans Don't Listen to Car Critics," *The Responsive Community*, Spring 1999, p. 47.
18. David Rieff, *Los Angeles: Capital of the Third World*, New York: Touchstone, 1991.
19. Clay McShane, *Down the Asphalt Path*, New York: Columbia University Press, 1994.
20. Jane Holtz Kay provides an extensive review of the costs of automobility in *Asphalt Nation*, New York: Crown, 1997.
21. Marshall Berman writes with great passion about what happened to the neighborhood of his youth because of the construction of the Cross-Bronx Expressway in New York City, in *All That Is Solid Melts into Air*, New York: Simon & Schuster, 1982. Lewis, Kay, and McShane, previously cited, also reflect on this issue.

22. See Richard Ingersoll, "The Death of the Street: The Automobile and Houston," in Jennings, *op. cit.*

23. Constance Perin, *Everything in Its Place*, Princeton, NJ: Princeton University Press, 1979. See especially Chs. 2 and 3.

24. Kenneth T. Jackson, *Crabgrass Frontier*, New York: Oxford Press, 1985.

25. Both Jackson and McShane develop this perspective.

26. Robert Fishman, *Bourgeois Utopias*, New York: Basic Books, 1987. See especially Ch. 4.

27. Quoted in Rieff, *op. cit.*, p. 45.

28. See the 1998 Sierra Club report, *The Dark Side of the American Dream*.

29. Robert J. Sampson, Stephen W. Raudenbush, Felton Earls, "Neighborhoods and Violent Crime: A Multilevel Study of Collective Efficacy," *Science Magazine*, August 15, 1997, pp. 918–924.

30. Ingersoll, *op. cit.*, p. 153.

31. Rieff, *op. cit.*, pp. 50–51.

6

Material Girls (and Boys)

When the market takes command of the culture, the ethical question changes from "How shall we live?" to "What do we want?" The explicit difference is in the loss of the sense of limits, the hesitation between the will and the act which can last forever in a society built on principle.

—Earl Shorris

People enjoy acquiring things, and they always have. Material objects can be a source of pleasure and delight, to say nothing of their ability to increase the ease of living. An automobile, for example, can be equally valued as a source of aesthetic pleasure and of functional utility. The desire for things is transcultural, suggesting that this attraction is linked to the genetic structure of human beings. The inherent appreciation for beauty—even as beauty is differently defined—the search for pleasure, and the continuing drive to control the environment, all attract people to the world of material objects.

Although this attraction may be genetically driven, it is not completely so. It is clear that some societies place a much higher value on accumulating material goods than do others, and thus this desire may be nurtured or discouraged. Nor is this variation in the attraction of acquisition and accumulation simply a function of economic organization. While people in capitalist countries are in general more acquisitive than people in noncapitalist ones, capitalist nations themselves vary significantly in this orientation. In any given society, therefore, the drive must be located within the context of other drives and interests that may conflict with a singular impulse for accumulation. All of the world's major religious traditions, for example, devote considerable attention to determining the right relationship between people and things. In short, whatever our genetic predispositions, some part of the interest in accumulating things is most certainly culturally driven.

In this book the term "materialism" is used, not in the classic Marxist sense, but simply to identify the pattern of beliefs that privileges the generation, possession, accumulation, and consumption of things. This pattern is animated by the conviction that well-being is largely a function of the quality and quantity of one's consumption. As we use this term, materialism reaches beyond the recognition that goods can produce pleasure. Pleasure itself is commodified, becoming something purchased in market exchanges. Such purchases extend beyond physical objects to include "lifestyle" acquisitions like the right vacation package or season tickets to prestigious events.

Everyone recognizes that goods and acquisition produce pleasure; and everyone recognizes that other, non-market exchanges—such as a walk in a park—do so as well. What is culturally interesting is the *weight* given to materialism as a source of pleasure in our society. In the United States, even a pristine activity such as a walk in the park may be reconfigured to accommodate materialist sensibilities, as one associates it with having the right walking shoes and outfit. One observer systematically chronicled the behavior of tour bus passengers as they arrived at a museum located in an urban center of the United States. He noted that one third of them, upon entering a museum foyer, find the gift shop, purchase an object—usually containing the museum logo—then return to the bus without ever entering the museum proper.[1] This commodification of pleasure is an example of materialism, as is the person who charges onto a scenic overlook of the Grand Canyon, quickly snaps a picture, rushes off to the next photo opportunity—all without experiencing the Canyon itself.

In the sense that we use the term, the United States is clearly the most materialist nation in the world—some claim in the history of the world. One might expect that, beyond a certain level, the desire to consume would abate, that an economic law of diminishing marginal utility would set in. It is reasonable to assume that the more one accumulates, the less attractive would be additional accumulation. Even children eventually learn, for example, that each additional piece of apple pie generates diminishing pleasure until a point is reached at which more pie is not attractive at all. In the world of general consumption, however, there is, so far, not much evidence for the existence of such a law. Or, perhaps this law is overwhelmed by other forces stimulating consumption. The data suggest that as Americans consume more, consumption grows in importance.

In 1987 the median response to the survey question "How much income per year would you say you (and your family) need to fulfill all of your dreams?" was $50,000. Ten years later, the median response had jumped to $90,000. In 1995, more than one quarter of Americans whose incomes *exceeded* $100,000 (placing them within the top 10 percent of income earners) reported that "I cannot afford to buy everything I really need," and about a fifth of them said, "I spend nearly all of my money on the basic necessities of life." While the number of people in households is shrinking, households themselves are growing larger—or at least heavier. In 1975, the moving industry reported that the average weight of interstate shipments of household goods was 5,645 pounds. Twenty years later the average weight of such shipments had jumped 30 percent, to 7,262 pounds.

The Bureau of Economic Analysis indicates that as incomes have grown, consumption has grown apace, and in recent years growth in consumption expenditures has exceeded income growth.[2] This is in part due to the fact that people are saving less. In 1995 the average American household saved 3.5 percent of its disposable income, about half the rate fifteen years before. By 1999 the national savings rate had dipped to an all-time low of 2.4 percent, according to the Commerce Department. Today, people are also more willing to go into debt to consume more—even though the consequences of this can sometimes be severe. In 1996 the number of personal bankruptcies was about 1 million. Three years later that number had jumped to 1.4 million, a figure three times greater than the number recorded in the early eighties. It should be noted that these bankruptcies occurred during a period of substantial economic prosperity. One major cause has been growing credit card debt. In 1997, the nation's households carried an average balance of $7,000 on their credit cards alone. In the prosperous nineties, the nation's revolving credit card debt more than doubled, according to the Federal Reserve Bank.

To a foreigner entering this country for the first time, our materialist orientation undoubtedly would be one of the most obvious cultural characteristics of the society. It might take some time and effort to understand how important the individualist ethic is to Americans, or to grasp the value that Americans place on mobility. Not so materialism. Because it is so imposingly physical, this characteristic is immediately obvious. Witness the ubiquitous, oversized transportation vehicles (fully loaded), gliding past endless billboards and beseeching store signs, even as the radio informs of still more purchasing possibilities; the vast, and vastly complicated, supermarkets where something as simple as buying chips is turned into a lengthy chain of decisions; the endless iteration of shopping malls, featuring total environments calibrated to the rhythms of consumption, capped by the crown jewel, MALL OF AMERICA, now an awe-inspiring vacation destination for many; the oversized homes, crammed to the rafters with the latest delights of the consumer society, including multiple television sets that in turn display images devoted to further acquisition; and the huge bins of trash filled weekly to clear the way for more things. These are only a few of the indicators of our national dedication to consumption that would be immediately apparent to a newly arrived visitor.

This American propensity has been satirized by a number of contemporary artists, one of the more interesting of whom is sculptor Nancy Rubins. Rubins, who now teaches art at UCLA, draws upon her childhood experience in Tennessee for inspiration. In the rural South, there is a long tradition of allowing junk to accumulate in yards rather than hauling it away. Rubins has become famous, or infamous, for creating huge public sculptures from discarded junk such as airplane parts, mobile homes, hot water heaters, toasters, mattresses, and the like. One of her works, located in a suburban shopping center in Chicago, was voted in a radio poll to be the "Ugliest Sculpture in Chicago." (Works by Miró and Picasso tied for second place.) Another of Rubins's works, commissioned by the Washington Project for the Arts, was ridiculed on CBS Evening News and so offended D.C. commuters on the Whitehurst Freeway that it was dismantled the moment its three-month permit expired. Evidently waste is not something of which Americans wish to be reminded.

This acquisitive orientation stretches far beyond any inherent value of the "things-in-themselves" to the province of culture. Any understanding of this orientation must be gleaned from a recognition of the role things play in our shared symbol system. In this chapter, we shall consider how materialism has become an integral aspect of American culture. How have Americans come to be so attracted to this kind of symbolic self-definition? In the next chapter, we will examine how materialism has expanded in recent years to occupy ever greater parts of everyday consciousness. We shall also consider the implications of this cultural value for political life.

MATERIALISM AND THE AMERICAN RELIGIOUS TRADITION

American religious communities have an ambivalent sense of the value of the material world. Many prominent religious leaders and organizations counsel against an overly strong interest in consumption, believing that it leads to the corruption of other values important to a good life. Others exalt consumption, arguing that it is a material sign of God's beneficence. Many a youngster has fidgeted through religious services wearing his or her "Sunday Best" in the belief that God would want him or her to "look nice" while worshipping. This ambivalence has deep historical roots.

It is somewhat surprising that the orientation toward consumption is in part connected to Puritanism, the religious tradition so influential in Colonial America. A central tenet of Puritanism, after all, was the rejection of the material world. To the Puritan, the lures of the earthly world were both ephemeral and destructive. John Bunyan's widely read seventeenth-century novel, *Pilgrim's Progress,* reflected this sensibility. One of the most harrowing parts of the Pilgrim's journey was having to pass through Vanity, a town dedicated to acquisition, which Bunyan stressed by noting that it held a year-round fair to market goods. As Christian and his companion, Faithful, passed through Vanity, they were bombarded with importunings to buy. When Christian and Faithful responded, "We buy Truth," they outraged the town's citizens, who beat and imprisoned them, and brought them to trial as enemies and disturbers of trade. Bunyan's message to his readers was clear and central: The world of commerce is seductive, but quite dangerous. This message conformed to the fundamental view of the Puritan that the world was a testing place, a temporal proving ground to illustrate one's worthiness for life in the permanent hereafter. Getting too comfortable in this temporal world was a distraction from life's essential purpose and, therefore, potentially lethal. In the colonies, the actual condition of life helped to reinforce this view. European immigrants coming to this continent had to hew life from a raw frontier, and this encouraged them to think about what was truly necessary in the material world. If many Europeans saw their compatriots in the New World as crude, ill-mannered primitives, colonists responded with a view that Europeans were effete and degenerate, made soft by over reliance on material "superfluities."

These inclinations notwithstanding, the colonies provided fertile soil for the seeds of materialism. The reality of the social structure in the New World tended to work against the Puritan ethos. In the rigid class structures of European societies, material accumulation was largely the province of the upper classes. The entrance of a European plebeian into the realm of consumption—assuming such entry were economically feasible—would represent a serious violation of social norms. Although integral to the colonial experience, social classes were much more fluid in America and the residue of feudalism far more distant. Gordon Wood chronicles the comparative weakness of the social class structure in Colonial America and shows how even that structure was undermined by the Revolution. One of the consequences of this was that people from lower social ranks were less inhibited about acquiring goods. This upset elite classes in America who, like their counterparts in Europe, regarded goods as an important source of social distinction.[3] One study locates the birth of the American Consumer in the period just after the Revolution and notes that by the 1800s America had become the most commercial nation on earth.[4]

Additionally, many religious European settlers carried with them images of the New World that stimulated a sensibility congenial to materialism. To these, the New World suggested Eden, the incarnation of the land of ease and plenty. Some Christian theologians believed, well into the seventeenth century, that Eden was an actual physical place that existed at the (unreachable) highest point on earth, and Columbus thought that his 1497 voyage to the New World, which took him to the coast of Venezuela, actually placed him in the neighborhood of Paradise.[5] Of course colonists did not literally believe they were entering Eden as they established their presence in the New World. Their complex sentiments, however, did leave room for predispositions that were not entirely sympathetic to the Protestant tradition of material rejection.

We now recognize, furthermore, that the Protestant tradition itself is more ambivalent regarding the material world than it at first seems. Max Weber is the most prominent of several scholars to unravel the paradox of the Protestant tradition fostering an immersion in the material world, even as it formally called for a withdrawal from that world. The psychological trauma resulting from unworthy sinners being judged by an inscrutable God led first to a drive for inner control, but ultimately to a drive for control of the environment as well. Puritans had a difficult time imagining that God would not smile on those who had chosen to follow Him. Success in the outside world became a sign of a righteous inner life, a reassurance that God was looking after the hopeful Christian.

There is a second sense in which this Protestant tradition is more closely connected to material accumulation than it at first seems. Perhaps the most fundamental belief of this tradition is the necessity of self-transformation. At the point of religious conversion, one recognizes one's sinful nature, yields oneself to God and is "born again." This is a gift requiring divine intervention, and it is an ecstatic experience. Protestant religious "awakenings," which since the eighteenth century have recurred periodically in American history, have often been accompanied by whoops and shouts, jubilant convulsions, and the like among converts. This loss of self-control provides visible evidence that God is indeed working in one's life. By its very nature therefore, this "other Protestant ethic" undermined commitments to control.[6] Thus, "letting go" in a frenzy of acquisition is less alien to this tradition, more widely known for its austerity, than it might seem.

One important study of the emergence of advertising in America connects the nineteenth-century appeal of the peddler, with his bag full of alluring items, and the patent medicine salesman, with his magical elixirs, to the deeply ingrained desire for self-transformation that was integral to the Protestant experience. The author notes that the emergence of advertising in the nineteenth century is closely linked to the idea of self-purification that is the essence of this tradition. The importance of cleanliness of the home and the body, the concern for plumbing and bowel regulation, are but a step away from spiritual quest. Advertisers both capitalized on and promoted ". . . the evangelical drive for what revivalists called 'entire and perfect sanctification' [a drive that] was becoming a largely secular project."[7]

THE SYMPATHETIC CULTURE

The development of a materialist orientation has also been encouraged and reinforced by the other aspects of the culture we considered in earlier chapters. For example, competition, mobility, and individualism offer both direct and indirect support for materialism. In the first case, the acquisition of goods became a direct, physical way to express each of these values. Material goods have obviously become a way to achieve social mobility. Buying a better home, a better car, even a better watch serve as cues both to the self and to others that one is moving up in the world. Acquisition is also a direct means of competition. People struggle to become the first in their reference group to have this or that product, after which others in the group often feel pressure to follow suit. Given this pressure, it is ironic that products are often marketed and acquired as expressions of individualism. People buy to bring distinction to themselves, to set themselves apart—at least from the humdrum masses. Through acquisition, a person can claim, "I am somebody."

It may be, however, that the most significant effects of individualism, competition, and mobility in promoting materialism are indirect. We have seen that this value matrix undercuts the sense of place, of belonging, of connection to others—in short, a sense of community. In its place, it nurtures a system of isolated loners struggling against others, constantly in motion. This world view deepens the sense of vulnerability that people feel, and it also undercuts identity. Implicit in the idea that we are not yet "all that we can be" is the sense that the current self is not so hot. The need for attachment and stasis is undervalued, as people are constantly encouraged to be something else. The never ending process of becoming certainly can be exciting, but it can be scary as well.

Thus, the needs generated in the culture proved to be fertile soil for the development of materialist values. People sought to allay the self-doubt generated in the larger culture through acquisition. By the dawn of the twentieth century, advertisers had learned to capitalize on and to extend these self-doubts. Product purchase was consciously promoted as a way to alleviate self-doubt, a ploy that is still integral to current marketing strategies. Ironically, the system extends self-doubt, even as purchasers seek its alleviation. In the constant search for more sales, modern advertising must *create* need. As prospective buyers are told that they will become better, more connected, or more highly regarded through product purchase, sellers must simultaneously impose and extend the sense that potential purchasers lack these qualities in their present states. Dissatisfaction is a necessary requisite for enhanced sales and is therefore both desired and cultivated by sellers.

These cultural tendencies can be illustrated when viewed through the prism of adolescence, that time of dramatic confrontation with the question of personal identity. This nether world between childhood and adulthood is often trying and painful. In adolescence, the child's sense of eternal fusion with a larger family structure gives way to the recognition of inevitable personal responsibility and identity that is characteristic of adulthood. It is at once highly appealing and very threatening—both to parents and to adolescents. Most of us probably remember adolescence as a time when we were on an emotional roller coaster. Moments of ecstasy are counterbalanced by moments of anger, fear, self-doubt, and cruelty. Parents often come to believe their children are beyond hope, and these fears are reciprocated by adolescents who believe that parents are irrelevant old fogies who will never understand young people. Given such tensions, it is hardly surprising that peer groups become extremely important to adolescents. The erosion of the sense of an eternal primary support system coupled with a not–yet–fully–formed–self can generate the kind of fear that drives teenagers to each other with an unusual sense of desperation. Being in the right group, being OK, is never more important nor more elusive.

When the sense of vulnerability generated by the cultural characteristics previously discussed are combined with adolescence, the resulting sentiments are a marketer's dream—and there is no more voracious consumer than the American teenager. The "neediness" that accompanies adolescence, the tentative nature of identity at that time, makes teenagers especially vulnerable to the importunings of the marketplace. The right look, the right style is of all-consuming importance precisely because identity is problematic. Parents sometimes learn, to their dismay, that even the right brands may not be good enough if they are purchased at the "wrong" stores, such as discount houses.

These characteristics of adolescence are well known. One useful way to think about advertising strategy in general is to recognize that its primary collective purpose is to arrest psychological development at adolescence—to extend, throughout the life cycle, the sense of material neediness that adolescents feel so intensely. To a substantial degree, these efforts have been successful.

THE TRANSFORMATION OF WORK

The Industrial Revolution transformed work, and one of the consequences of this transformation was to encourage acquisitiveness. Today, the patterns of work that emerged with developing industrialism are accepted with little controversy. They are commonplace, seeming simply to be part of the way things are. In the nineteenth century, however, the social and political consequences of work patterns in the emergent manufacturing system were a significant concern both to workers and to intellectuals in the United States.[8] Jeffersonians and their heirs were especially alarmed. They believed that the great national experiment in self-government could only succeed if its citizens were infused with what was called civic virtue. Civic virtue was the capacity to think beyond narrow self-interest, to habitually render reasoned judgments about the best interests of society as a whole. More than anything else, it was believed, civic virtue required personal autonomy and independence. Dependency undercut democracy by promoting a narrow, self-interested politics.

Jeffersonians feared industrial work patterns would subvert the foundation for the emerging and fragile democratic society. They believed that yeoman farmers were essential to a vibrant democracy because the self-sufficient, autonomous lifestyle of farming had the fortuitous consequence of cultivating civic virtue. It provided what modern political scientists would call appropriate political socialization for a democratic society. In contrast, Jeffersonians saw the nascent industrial economic system as a threat, worrying that its dependent work relationships would generate people who were not up to the demands of democracy. Jefferson was attracted to the huge Louisiana Purchase in part because he hoped to insure that the United States would remain a predominantly agrarian society. The movement attacking "wage slavery" in the pre–Civil War North was based upon this republican belief that economic and political independence went hand-in-hand. After the war, a populist movement fought a bitter, rear-guard action against the industrial tide.[9]

It would be silly to romanticize pre-industrial worklife. Typically farmers carved out a hardscrabble, and short, life with long hours of backbreaking labor. But the rural way of life did have its rewards, and the appeals of materialism cannot be fully understood without a recognition of what was lost as the society industrialized. The rural life did generate a sense of autonomy. People had a measure of control over their lives, organizing their own work routines themselves. Work was an extension of home life, with all members of the family except the very youngest having serious responsibilities. Meager as it often was, there was at least a visible emotional return for labor. What was sowed, if the weather cooperated, was also reaped. There was also a sense of community in this austere life. People banded together to assist each other in important tasks and for mutual protection against the ravages of nature.

In the new industrial order, things were different. Some became fabulously wealthy and others eased into the new middle class. For the majority, however, the sense of vulnerability increased. The loss of control over one's life was palpable, as people worked long hours for low pay under conditions which were profoundly demeaning. As workers sold their time to large organizations, time itself was transformed. The clock became a major enemy, with lives now shaped according to its divisions. People could be thrown out of work at the whim of some boss, because of injury, or as the result of unpredictable economic panic. Hierarchy, an organizational mode characterized by dependence and inequality, dominated the workplace. Productive work, which had been the foundation of social identity, often seemed irrelevant to any larger purpose beyond personal survival. This increasing sense of personal incoherence was reinforced by the anonymity of a fluid urban life, wherein people felt as if they were specks "in an amorphous mass of similar specks."[10] Work, which historically had a larger, integrative purpose, was now experienced by many as a form of emasculation.

These conditions spawned the American labor movement. Some elements of this movement, including the more radical Populists and unions such as the Industrial Workers of the World, challenged the legitimacy of corporate hierarchy and control. The IWW, or "Wobblies," organized workers around the principle of "one big union." The new order, Wobblies believed, produced two classes of people: honest workers of all sorts, and a class of greedy profiteers who illicitly co-opted the fruits of labor. Writing in the 1880s, Henry Demerest Lloyd argued that the spirit of democracy in the United States included the "inalienable right of the people to own and operate, at their option, any or all of the wealth they create."[11]

Unlike the labor movement in Europe, however, which stimulated the rise of major socialist parties throughout that continent, American labor radicals were never ascendant. For a variety of political, cultural, and social reasons, the central tendencies of the labor movement in this country were much more conservative. Management and owners strongly resisted even this more conservative sort of union activity, however. Labor organizers were summarily fired and blacklisted. Goons were hired to break strikes and picket lines. Violence was a frequent by-product of labor disputes. Well into the twentieth century, the power of the state, including the courts and the military, was brought to bear on behalf of owners and managers against workers. Early labor history in the United States is marked by a series of bitter and often bloody struggles.

In the end, neither side was entirely successful. Labor and corporate capital eventually reached a tacit bargain, which has been called capitalism's great compromise. On one hand, labor unions won a measure of legitimacy. They worked for concessions on wages, benefits, and greater workplace safety—although these were often themselves the product of intense struggle. On the other hand, labor ceased agitating for fundamental worker control of the production process and ratified the legitimate place of owners. Eventually owners came to understand that increased worker buying power led to new markets for increased productive capacity.

It is important to understand the significance of the concessions made by labor in this compromise. Workers did gain in a number of ways, but the compromise also meant that the possibilities for satisfaction in work were greatly diminished. Unions managed to reduce worker dependency somewhat, but they could not create autonomy. The compromise ratified hierarchy and inequality in the workplace and conferred legitimacy to managers in making key corporate decisions. In many cases workers were treated with kindness, but it was not the kindness that grew out of a sense of equality and fraternity. It was more akin to the kindness of the benevolent despot in which the reciprocating sentiment was expected to be gratitude. The compromise left workers with little choice but to seek satisfaction away from the job. The emerging world of mass advertising promised that this satisfaction could be obtained through the consumption of entertainment and goods.

Advertisers recognized that the fun gleaned from consumption was derived in part because everyday life was so dreary. One advertising copywriter somewhat arrogantly summarized this sense in 1925:[12]

> In spite of his seeming sophistication, the American citizen is naive, fresh, essentially childlike, full of generous enthusiasms and the capacity for wonderment. His everyday life is pretty dull. Get up—eat—go to work—eat—go to bed. But his mind is constantly reaching out beyond this routine. This is one of the reasons the American is such a great fiction reader—movie goer—talking machine and radio fan. He compensates for the routine of to-day by the expectation of what his life is to be to-morrow.

Consumption became a way to obscure one's dependent social class position. As historian Stuart Ewen has noted, social class position has both objective and subjective components.[13] The objective component is the location of a given individual according to publicly identified criteria. The subjective component to social class position is the place where an individual locates him or herself. In the subjective world, appearance is more important than reality. If the objective indications were that a given individual was a social inferior, the world of consumption could create the subjective appearance of social status and dignity. Perhaps it was even possible for appearance to overwhelm reality. Ewen attributes the emergence of "style" to this sensibility, and argues that the "compulsory consumption of images" now stands at the heart of the American Dream. In short, consumption confers status to a worker desperate for reassurance. Chapter One discussed how the extensive use of symbol systems was a defining human characteristic. We use symbols to construct meaning. Ewen calls the assembling of the commodity self that occurred at the end of the last century "symbolic democratization," a process that has intensified in this century.

The emergence of style as defining the self is a central theme in Theodore Dreiser's classic turn-of-the-century novel *Sister Carrie*, a sharp commentary on life in the newly emergent industrial order. For Dreiser's characters, appearance is everything; in fact, no one is anything *but* appearance. The characters seem like mannequins, completely devoid of any qualities that would make the reader sympathetic to them. Dreiser portrays a society that is Jefferson's worst nightmare. Pages are devoted to describing how the successful "look," the quality of the cloth in a coat, the gradations of footwear. It is such empty things, rather than any kind of internal qualities, that distinguish social levels. Rising and falling in this society are matters of whimsy. The novel's amorality created a stir in social leadership circles of the day, and Dreiser had considerable trouble getting it published. Yet Dreiser saw clearly some of the costs of the emerging industrial order.

Finally, the extension of mass consumption can be seen as an effort to solve the new "needs of both owners and workers in the emerging industrial order." On one hand, huge profits could be made from the capacity to mass produce goods. In order to sell these goods, however, it was necessary to produce mass markets. The function of advertising inevitably became to generate consumers in prodigious numbers. On the other hand, an astute cultural critic has forcefully argued that the penchant for mass consumption must also be seen as a function of the larger pattern of dependence, disorientation, and loss of control growing out of the system of mass production in industrializing society.[14] In short, "consumerism is only the other side of the degradation of work," which is why it flourished so substantially in the latter part of the nineteenth century.

If this assessment is correct, it could also help explain the surge of consumerism that has accompanied "post-industrial" America. Although much of the work of the older industrial era was emasculating, it nevertheless provided an identity of sorts. There was an element of stability to worklife. In part because of the struggle of worker organizations, workers were able to gain a measure of security. They could think of a lifetime of work that would provide decent living conditions for their families, followed by a retirement that, when eventually coupled with Social Security, promised a measure of dignity. If work failed to provide essential human dignity, at least workers knew how they fit in the larger scheme of things. They could point to the products they helped to make. They were steel workers or automobile makers.

In Chapter Five we noted the argument that the swirling post-industrial world makes even this form of identity increasingly problematic. What one actually does in one's worklife is more ambiguous and harder to explain to others. Worklife is much more fluid. "Temporary work" is now one of the fastest growing job categories. Even in an era of widespread prosperity and growing profits, corporations merge, downsize, or move overseas, leaving workers throughout the job hierarchy in the lurch. It is hardly surprising that workers today express far less loyalty to their employers than they once did—why shouldn't they?

   Polls show that, even during the time of remarkably low unemploy-ment in the late nineties, workers were increasingly uncertain and nerv-ous about the lack of stability in their work lives. In a speech to the American Council on Education, Federal Reserve Chairman Alan Greenspan underscored the trends. In 1981, during the deepest recession since the Great Depression of the thirties, International Survey Research published the results of a national survey indicating that 12 percent of American workers feared losing their jobs. In contrast the same research firm noted that in prosperous 1999, 37 percent of the work force was con-cerned about job loss, a threefold increase.[15] Perhaps this brave new world of economic insecurity has some social benefit. There are those who would make such an argument. But, whatever the benefit, it is also likely to intensify the search for identity and recovery of the self.

   Ironically, advertising rhetorically appropriated citizens' memories of the pre-industrial past, including the nurturing household and com-munity life, in an effort to make the products generated by the new system of labor more appealing.[16] Bucolic and traditional themes were regularly evoked and connected to product consumption. The process whereby cor-porations promise that the values systematically assaulted by the *pro-duction* of goods and services can be restored by their *consumption* is now standard operating procedure.

   Watching a single evening of Monday Night Football,[17] I noted some of the fears and longings of consumers that commercials sought to iden-tify, reinforce, and exploit. "Will you remember me?" (AT&T). "You need to defend yourself against a world of predators" (First Union Bank). "Where do you want to go today?" (Microsoft). "You're in control" (Sprint). "A guide who knows the way" (Prudential). "Man can be judged by more than who he is" (Ford). "So you won't feel alone" (State Farm). "Your ticket to freedom" (Southwest Airlines). "No limit to where it can take you" (Chrysler). "It's about freedom. Now you're in control" (Schwab). "Be everywhere you want to be" (Visa). "Your life is full of worries. Your car shouldn't be" (Chevro-let). Thus, the products of a system of work that also creates anxiety and a diminished sense of self in its workers are offered to workers as means for reclaiming the self. The problem is reinvented as the solution.

TELEVISION

The advent of television has had a dramatic impact on the acceleration of acquisitiveness over the last half of the twentieth century. As noted in Chapter Three, Americans are great television watchers. In surveys, Amer-icans report that it is their major leisure time activity. It is no accident that shopping ranks second on the list of leisure time activities, for the two are integrally connected. A recent study has documented the correla-tion between TV watching and consumption. The more people watch TV, the more things they buy. With justification, television has been called "the umbilical cord of the consumer society."[18]

Most people think of television simply as entertainment—and free entertainment at that. This is not surprising, since this is how television fare is represented. The fact that TV is fundamentally an economic enterprise is obscured. But American television is a business, and its business is, most simply, selling audiences to advertisers. In exchange for licenses to use the public airwaves, the government does establish broad and vague parameters regarding taste, and it requires a minimal commitment to some public interest programming. So long as they remain within these broad boundaries of acceptability, TV stations are free to do whatever they deem necessary to maximize profits.

No other television system in the world rivals the American system in its single-minded devotion to commercial interests. In some countries advertising has been banned; in others it is more constricted. It may be surprising to learn that the television systems of other nations differ from our own. Americans are so conditioned by their own experience that it is hard to imagine television being any other way. The constant commercial interruptions of programming, the altering of rules for athletic events to allow more time for commercials, the seamless transitions in which Olympic champions glide from award ceremonies into McDonald's for an order of fries, all these appear not as Coen Brothers outtakes, but as part of a natural television world.

It was not always thus. In the early days of radio, most stations were owned by colleges and universities.[19] The development of private stations stimulated a concern for profits, but turning the airwaves over to commercial interests was initially quite controversial. Many thought advertising on radio was a desecration, and legislation was introduced in Congress to ban it. As Secretary of Commerce in the 1920s, even the conservative Herbert Hoover expressed reservations about the propriety of advertising on radio. Despite this concern, there was never a serious national debate over the proper administration of the airwaves as there was in Canada, for example. Instead, private interests won a war of attrition. In the beginning, advertisers were careful not to offend public sensibilities. The earliest advertisers, such as Browning-King, simply attached their names to programs. When specific ads emerged initially, they appeared only between programs. The current reality, in which viewers are swamped with commercial advertisements, is the product of a long evolution.

Television's pervasiveness is such that its form seems ineluctable. Both the experience of other countries and our own history, however, suggest that our current system is the result of political and social decisions we have made. The point is neither to decry nor exalt these decisions, but to recognize their significance, as the resulting system reverberates through our culture. What is relevant for our purposes is to indicate television's impact on consumption. For three reasons, television is an unrivaled tool for marketers.

First, television has achieved a level of social penetration that is unprecedented historically and unrivaled by other mediums. Television is unique in that almost everyone watches it, at least some of the time. TV ownership is virtually universal, and today 60 percent of American homes have three or more TV sets.[20] Its vast audience includes literati and illiterates alike. This provides the marketer with extraordinary choice. A huge market can be reached at a single moment by advertising in a popular time slot, or during a heavily watched special event like the Super Bowl or Barbara Walters's interview of Monica Lewinsky.[21] But the vastness of the audience also allows for highly focused ads targeting selected regional and demographic groups. Sellers can select shows that are geared to teenagers, to men or women, to families, to elderly insomniacs, and so forth.

A second reason television is such an effective advertising instrument is that, unlike the major print alternatives, it plays to a captive audience. Reading an advertisement in a newspaper or magazine requires an affirmative decision on the part of the reader. Whole sections of newspaper advertising may be ignored by those not interested in shopping. Television advertising is much more seductive. TV lures the viewer into commercials, in part by inertia, in part because ads are always paced more rapidly than other kinds of content, and in part because programming is calibrated around commercials. Dramatic shows are paced to maximize commercial efficiency; the rules of sport are altered to be more accommodating as well. Even the most ardent channel surfer cannot avoid all TV advertising. It is too ubiquitous, often occurring during the program itself, and its timing too well coordinated by networks. It is graphically and temporally designed to attract viewer attention as well.

Developments within modern capitalism have helped to make American television the unrivaled leader of advertising. The moral underpinning of capitalism has always been its assertion of the dignity and worth of the individual. The assumption of individual rationality emanates from this conviction. The virtue of capitalism, as its theorists see it, is its core conviction that individuals have the ability to make well-reasoned decisions about what is best for them and ought to be allowed to do so. Market transactions allow this process to unfold. This conviction, of course, recognizes a legitimate role for advertising. After all, consumers need product knowledge in order to make rational decisions about purchases, and advertising is an important way to supply such knowledge. Thus advertising can be seen as an ally of reason, even of enlightenment. Undoubtedly, some advertising works in this fashion.

As capitalism has developed, however, this moral foundation has become more tenuous. Advertising, which began as an ally of reason in that it provided information necessary for consumers to make rational choices, has become increasingly preoccupied with subverting reason. This development is a consequence of the internal logic of capitalism. Profit maximization and competition lead corporations to make increasingly emotional claims about products and to attach products to sentiments (such as sexual desire) having nothing to do with the products themselves. In short, advertisers are logically led to an interest in *subverting* rationality. The information function of advertising was always a means to the primary end—the sale of products. If products can be more effectively sold by nonrational emotional appeals, the information function will give way to them. In this new reality, the rational individual, who originally was fundamental to the moral foundation of capitalism, becomes the problem, the entity who must be undone.

This movement toward sentiment in the advertising industry elevates the significance of television, for television is the unparalleled medium of sentiment. Novels, of course, can be extraordinarily sentimental, but because their form is entirely literary, authors must labor to build the sentiment. No medium approaches the ability of television to create sentiment in the small packets required by advertising. This can be seen in the way television ads move us. While magazine ads are difficult to recall, for example, everyone can recall dozens of memorable TV ads. People buy theater tickets to see a compendium of the best television ads of the previous year. TV commercials are regularly integrated into everyday lives through humming jingles, borrowing quips, and the like. For many, the ads on the Super Bowl rival interest in the game itself. Post-game news stories now regularly analyze these ads, discussing the winners and the losers of the ad competition just as sports analysts discuss the game itself.

Television is unrivaled in its ability to demonstrate products and resolve problems in such a way that things invariably come out perfectly—all in thirty seconds. One observer of the market and culture puts the matter succinctly:[22]

> Before television, the salesman, who mediated between desire and information, was able to affect only a part of life. He worked at what is now called the point of sale. His effect was largely limited to manipulating information in the brief encounter. Television operated differently, moving back from the point of sale into the processes of imagination and desire. As television mediated between Americans and more and more of reality, it had a greater opportunity to affect the customer, to change desire, than any previous salesman, including the trickster in Eden.

As significant as advertising on television is, economist Juliet P. Schor believes that television programming may be even more important in stimulating consumer desire.[23] She shows that the long-established American penchant for consumption started zooming upward in the eighties. Begin-

ning at that time, a culture of upscale spending emerged, which she identifies as "the new consumerism." Analysts have long recognized that patterns of consumption are connected to reference groups. People tend to
want what others with whom they identify have. This phenomenon, which
sociologists in the forties labeled "keeping up with the Joneses," exerts
pressure to consume. In the past, however, the Joneses were the folks next
door. Because neighborhoods tend to be economically similar, the Joneses
were likely to be people whose economic circumstances approximated those
living near them. In Schor's phrase, the reference groups with whom we
compared ourselves were horizontal. The fact that reference groups were
comprised largely of people who were economically similar served as a
modest brake on consumption.

Schor argues that this has now changed. One of the distinctive characteristics of the new consumerism is that reference groups have become
vertical and now stretch across economic and social class. In part, she
attributes this change to the surge of married women into the work force
that began in the seventies. This meant the "workplace replaced the coffee
klatch and the backyard barbecue as locations of social contact." Inevitably
the workplace has become a source of information about who was buying
and doing what. But the workplace exposes people to a wider economic
spectrum than does the neighborhood, especially in white collar occupa-
tions. Hence the reference groups became more vertical.

Schor also recognizes that television has been an important source
of vertical pressure, probably more important than changes in the workplace. Because television delivers huge audiences, sellers whose target
may be millionaires nevertheless expose their wares to those with modest incomes as well, thus exerting upward buying pressures on them.
Lexus, for example, might advertise on a popular sitcom time slot because
many wealthy people would watch the show, even though the vast majority of the audience are people of more modest means. In contrast, they
would not bother to advertise in *Popular Mechanics*.

Beyond this, the content of television, its programming, creates vertical reference groups. The doctors, lawyers, psychiatrists, and other characters of prime time TV, overwhelmingly dress stylishly and live
commodiously in a world of material pleasure. Often this is completely
disconnected from the supposed "reality" of the show. The characters on
the popular sitcom "Friends," for example, manage to live in Manhattan and
to dine sumptuously at the table of consumption despite the fact that they
are mostly occupationally struggling twenty-somethings.

Even if the main characters are not particularly stylish, other characters are there for contrast. In *NYPD Blue*, Detective Sipowicz (Dennis
Franz) exists in stark contrast to the other main leads on the show. Against
Sorenson (Ricky Scroeder) or any of the major female leads, his bad hair-
cut practically screams at the viewer. We may like him, but we know he is

a slob. It is obvious that people do identify with television's characters. A "new look" for an important television personality can stimulate an economic ripple throughout the economy.

The new consumerism is made more problematic by the fact that it emerged as the wealthiest 10 percent of the population began to accumulate ever greater proportions of total national wealth. Thus, the more diverse reference groups that accompany the new consumerism are more economically diverse than ever, exacerbating the pressure on middle- and working-class folks who struggle to keep up with the wealthier people with whom they now identify.

A few years ago a friend mailed me a letter of solicitation he had received from Corestates Visa. He was invited into a special realm of privilege, to be singled out as one who held this top-of-the-line card. This card would "immediately identify" him as a person who was both worthy of respect and wise—his wisdom being made palpable by the fact that he chose to carry this "prestigious" card. What is interesting about this appeal is that it is less about commodities than it is about *access* to them. My friend was assured he would be revered by others simply because he held the key to the kingdom. "Hello. My name is _____. See my Corestates Visa? I can buy things. Therefore, I am."

In this chapter we have seen that, from uncertain roots, acquisition has become integral to American culture. In modern society materialism is expanding. Its domain is reaching into areas that have not been, heretofore, significantly under its influence, so that today growing proportions of everyday consciousness come under its sway. This transformation has great political consequence. It is to this process that we now turn.

NOTES

1. This study is cited in Juliet B. Schor, *The Overspent American*, New York: Basic Books, 1998, p. 48.
2. The income, savings, spending, and bankruptcy trends reported here were synthesized from three sources: *The Policy News and Information Service* report, "'Tis the Season: Holiday Consumer Trends," December 20, 1998, www.policy.com; A Bureau of Economic Analysis News Release, November 25, 1998; and Schor, *op. cit.,* p. 20. Data from 1999 are taken from "Americans Deep in Debt," Carlos Sadovi, *Chicago Sun-Times*, July 12, 1999, p. 1.
3. Gordon S. Wood, *The Radicalism of the American Revolution*, New York: Vintage, 1991.
4. Earl Shorris, *A Nation of Salesmen*, New York: Avon Books, 1994, p. 66.
5. T.J. Jackson Lears, *Fables of Abundance*, New York: Basic Books, 1994, p. 27.
6. See Lears, *op.cit.*, pp. 46–56, for an interesting discussion of "the other Protestant Ethic." The phrase itself was coined by sociologist Colin Campbell.
7. Lears, *op. cit.,* p. 166.

8. See Chs. 5 and 6 of Michael Sandel, *Democracy's Discontent*, Cambridge: Harvard University Press, 1996, for an excellent review of these issues.

9. See Lawrence Goodwyn, *The Populist Moment*, New York: Oxford University Press, 1978.

10. Lears, *op. cit.,* p. 55.

11. Originally cited in Robert Holsworth and J. Harry Wray, *American Politics and Everyday Life*, New York: Macmillan, 1987, p. 28.

12. Quoted in Lears, *op. cit.,* p. 231.

13. Stuart Ewen, *All Consuming Images*, New York: Basic Books, 1988, pp. 62–64, 78–79.

14. Christopher Lasch, *The Minimal Self*, New York: W.W. Norton, 1984, p. 27.

15. These figures were taken from a speech delivered by Alan Greenspan to the American Council on Education on February 16, 1999.

16. Lears, *op. cit.,* pp. 384–385.

17. The Monday Night Football Game that was assessed occurred on December 28, 1998.

18. The study correlating TV watching and shopping is contained in Schor, *op.cit.* To my best knowledge, the "umbilical cord" phrase was coined by sociologist Todd Gitlin.

19. These historical observations are taken from Erik Barnouw's definitive study on the subject, *A History of Broadcasting*, New York: Oxford University Press, 1970.

20. Data were gathered in a Kaiser Family Foundation Report, *Kids & Media @thenewmillennium*, Victoria J. Rideour, Ulla G. Foehr, Donald F. Roberts, Mollyann Brodie, November, 1999.

21. For the 20/20 Walters/Lewinsky interview, for example, ABC was able to quadruple the rate it normally charged advertisers. A thirty-second advertising slot on the 2000 Super Bowl went for $3 million.

22. Shorris, *op. cit.,* p. 88.

23. Schor, *op. cit.,* Ch. 1.

7

The Imperialism
of Consumption Values

*The manifest destiny of American business is not a matter of occupying vast
tracts of empty land, but of seeking out new frontier territories of the mental
and the built environments in which to plant their brand-label flags. With
pioneering fervor they stalk the last few stretches of logo-free America, hoping to get a piece of the rapidly filling market-niche frontier with a new round
of "place-based" or "out-of-home" advertising. . . . With imperial arrogance
advertisers feel that if there is space in society that is not currently being used
to sell a product, then it is theirs to exploit.*

—Tom Vanderbilt

Most Americans are familiar with the concept of imperialism. We are introduced to it early in schools, as we begin to study history and politics—
doubtless because the United States was born out of resistance to an
imperialist power. We know that an imperialist nation seeks to extend its
control beyond its widely recognized political boundaries, to geographic
areas where political and military organization is weak. Such expansion is
justified on the grounds that it is both in the national interest of the imperialist power and also part of the "right" order of things. Imperialist nations
generally argue that the conquered territory substantially benefits from
the new relationship. The imperial power provides protection, and helps

bring the conquered territory into "modernity," by encouraging the adoption of implicitly "superior" religious, social, and economic institutions. Thus, in addition to being expansionist, the imperial power is also hegemonic, expending considerable energy to fuse its own consciousness with that of the conquered peoples. It wants them to recognize and accept the benefits of the new relationship.

The concept of imperialism is characteristically used to explain relations between nation states. However, within our own borders, something like this process has been occurring with respect to the cultural characteristic of materialism. In recent decades the national commitment to materialism has grown substantially, as the values of acquisition are increasingly embedded in our consciousness. As these values expand their dominion, they edge toward hegemony. Conquered spheres are reshaped according to the values and assumptions of materialism. These appear, not as social contrivance, but as part of the natural order of things.

GROWING NUMBER OF ADS

One way the expansion of materialist values can be seen is simply to recognize the growing number of ads to which Americans are exposed daily. In the pursuit of profit, the national media system—including newspapers, magazines, TV, radio, and the Internet—cedes ever more space and time to advertising. In Chapter Six we noted that advertising on the airwaves was initially controversial, but grew to be commonplace. Nevertheless, in television's first thirty years, the Federal Communications Commission, the government agency that allocates licenses allowing stations to operate over public airwaves, limited the amount of time television stations could commit to advertising. Because air waves are a public resource, stations are required by law to operate in the "public interest, convenience, and necessity." Until the eighties, the FCC used its "public interest" mandate to limit the amount of prime time stations could sell to advertisers to twelve minutes per hour.

The FCC commissioners appointed during the more laissez faire era of President Reagan believed the amount of time sold to advertisers should be determined by the market, not the government, and dropped the prime time limitation. Since then, television advertising has been growing. In drafting this chapter, I randomly selected a few hours of television and assessed the time devoted to advertising. In prime time, eighteen minutes of an hour were given to advertising. During this time, the network ran forty-six ads and network promotions. An hour-long late night show gave nineteen minutes to advertising, while an hour of morning programming devoted twenty minutes and thirty seconds of an hour to advertising.[1]

A comprehensive study of newspapers noted that between 1940 and

1980, the proportion of newspaper space devoted to advertising grew from 40 to 65 percent.[2] Anyone picking up a Sunday paper these days would find it hard to believe that the proportions have not grown further since that study. Popular magazines, from "news" magazines like *Time* and *Newsweek* to "personality" magazines like *People*, to "lifestyle" magazines such as *Esquire* and *Cosmopolitan* are bursting with ads. Today it is not uncommon to leaf through many pages of ads in magazines without encountering an article of any sort. In contrast to print and early electronic media, the Internet has developed without any sense of the impropriety of ads. From its genesis, advertisements have bombarded anyone making use of the Iinternet's services.

COMMERCIALIZATION OF NEW SPHERES

The increase in the raw number of ads to which we are daily exposed is one dimension of the imperialism of consumer society. A second dimension is exemplified by the 1999 Papal visit to Mexico. Because such visits are expensive, the Catholic Church and the host country normally work out some agreement to share costs. This visit broke with that tradition, and for the first time, a Pope visited a country under the aegis of corporate sponsorship. More than two dozen corporations paid for the right to be an "official sponsor" of the visit. Several U.S. companies with economic interests in Mexico, including Pepsi and Frito-Lay, were prominent among the sponsors. Frito-Lay placed devotional messages and stamp-sized pictures of the Pope into bags of Ruffles potato chips. Huge Pepsi billboards went up along Mexico's highways, citing the words of John Paul from a previous visit: "Mexico, Always Faithful." The signs added: "Pepsi—official sponsor of the Fourth Visit of His Holiness John Paul II to Mexico." Church officials in Mexico justified the sponsorship, arguing that it made the visit affordable. Consistent with hegemonic framing, this commercialization was seen as benign. But it is an imposition of consumer values into a sphere of consciousness where it had not previously existed. The Christian faithful were encouraged to think of His Holiness and product acquisition simultaneously. Now that this Rubicon has been crossed, who knows what lies ahead? Perhaps a Papal miter with a Nike swoosh.[3]

This incident illustrates the general process that seems destined to recast all experience into occasions for consumption. The heightened priority of the values of consumption, the commodification of spheres that had once been relatively independent of commercialization, has reached epidemic proportions. Virtually any social sphere could be used to highlight this process. We have selected three: leisure time, childhood, and sport.

HOLIDAYS AND LEISURE TIME

Holidays and leisure time once offered respite from the world of work. That was their point. Today, however, holidays and leisure have undergone a "makeover." Instead of respite and relief, they are increasingly reconstructed as occasions for consumption. So total has been this assault that commercials now carry the message that weekends and evenings are made *possible* by this or that product. Jogging, playing tennis or basketball, even a walk in the woods is now integrally connected to an array of products, and topped off with the right beer or café latte. Americans are encouraged to think of shopping as a leisure time activity, and the most intense periods of shopping are holidays such as Thanksgiving, Labor Day, and Christmas. Increasingly, the point of holidays is to consume, and commercial interests lobby Congress for the designation of "special" days, the better to hock their wares.

"Holiday" comes from the medieval term "holy day," a day that was set aside for worship, celebration, and respite from work. It is not simply that leisure time and holidays no longer provide the respite from work that they once did. As time away from work is increasingly commodified, people are bound more closely to the workplace. They must work harder to provide the funds that commodity consumption requires. Thus many seek overtime, or second seasonal jobs, in order to "celebrate" Christmas appropriately.

One can see the absorption of leisure into the aesthetic of materialism by considering a favorite leisure time activity of Americans—movie-going. Movies have always been a form of consumption, but once this consumption consisted merely of entertainment and diversion. As this entertainment form has developed, however, its connection to broader consumption patterns has deepened. Today movies offer far less respite from the defining American task of product consumption than they once did. The nation's multiplexes now regularly run ads before the movies begin. The era when movies, out of a sense of probity, avoided showing identifiable commercial products has been replaced by a new reality in which producers are paid by companies to integrate products into films. The movie industry spawns a growing array of products—books, posters, hats, T-shirts, accessories, sound tracks, action figures, video games, and the like—that stimulate attachment, promotion, and greater consumption. Today newscasts dutifully report the highest weekly grossing films, thus underscoring what is socially significant about them.

One critic notes that the most distinctive genre of the American film industry, the spectacular special-events epic, presents to the viewing public "consumption as spectacle." Each year the industry produces films such as *The Titanic*, *Godzilla*, *Star Wars*, and *The Fugitive*, that spare no expense in creating and destroying costly sets and carefully built constructions. Industry executives hype the costly destruction in trade papers and the popular media. Other films, not totally committed to epic destruction, often feature memorable scenes, such as car chases, that terminate in spectacular destruction. In these cinematic "towering infernos," things are literally consumed before our eyes. The *point* of such films seems to be to spend money, their huge production costs simultaneously demanding and legitimizing the attention of the movie-going public.[4]

GROWING INTO THE CONSUMER CULTURE

A few decades ago, childhood was regarded as a time of innocence, a stage of life when one was free of larger social responsibilities. No more. Perhaps taking a cue from developmental psychology, which shows that early experience tends to be foundational, corporations now seek to induct children into the consumer society during their earliest years of childhood. This induction is made easier by the fact that children watch so much television. A 1999 study of children and the media by the Kaiser Family Foundation reported that more than half of all children have TV sets in their own room, and that they recognize brand names as early as age two.[5]

The induction process is especially stimulated by children's TV. There have always been ads on children's television, a fact which is in itself shameful. (The major function of such ads is to get children to nag their parents into buying products—even harmful products, like highly-sugared cereals.) Selling to children on TV has moved to a higher level of sophistication, however. A growing proportion of program "content" is simply a pretext for marketing goods. Children's television characters, story lines, and market products are created simultaneously, so that the products are immediately available for purchase. On such programs, distinguishing advertising time and program time makes no sense. A child watching two hours of morning television is, in effect, watching two hours of commercial marketing.

Famous brands have extended their lines to include children. Nike features infant shoes in size one emblazoned with their name and logo. Stores such as "Baby Gaps," "My First Sony," and "Baby Guess" spirit children along the consumer highway. Mattel and Mastercard have ratcheted the process up a notch with the addition of "Cool Shoppin' Barbie" to the famous doll line. This version of the doll comes with a Mastercard in her hand and is sold with cash register, clothes, shoes, and "see-thru" shopping bag. The results of these efforts are palpable. Teachers now report that, in the earliest grades of elementary school, children are quite conscious of designer lines.

The establishment of American Girl Place represents a new milestone in the commercialization of childhood. Growing out of a successful doll catalogue business, the first American Girl Place was opened in Chicago in time for the 1998 Christmas season. It has been a business bonanza. Located just around the corner from Chicago's Magnificent Mile, the poshest shopping area in the midwest, AGP is a worthy training ground for young, upscale shoppers. It is not easy to say exactly what AGP *is*. Based around six theme dolls, it is far more than a doll shop. Housed in an elegant three story minimall, it is more than this as well. AGP is totalitarian, that is, a total concept in which child and commodity are fused.

On one hand, the little girls who come to AGP are deeply immersed in the world of commodities. The products that one may buy for a "starter" doll seem limitless and include homes, vehicles, furniture, accessories, additional outfits, holiday ensembles, skin and hair care products (for the dolls), luggage, and more. There are even Bitty Baby dolls, with their own line of accessories, for the dolls themselves. All of these are displayed in well-lighted glass enclosures. In front of the cases are rows of tickets placed at child-appropriate heights. As the child cruises these floors, she simply pulls the tickets of the desired products and takes them to some adult or store representative.

On the other hand, the children themselves are commodified. AGP has a significant line of girls' clothing modeled after the clothing the dolls wear, so that children can "Dress like your American Girl Doll—Today!" Children and their identically dressed dolls frequent the shopping corridors of AGP. Lines form at a popular photo booth where, for a price, a girl and her doll become "models" for the corporation, appearing on a souvenir copy of American Girl Magazine.

The ground floor of AGP is designed to resemble a museum. The six basic dolls are keyed to a particular period of U.S. history. Each has a little book telling the doll's "story." The museum-like cases that house the dolls are filled with consumables that are "appropriate" to each era, all of which may be selected by pulling a ticket. The mantra of the sales personnel in this section of the store is that, by making children more familiar with historic eras, AGP "educates as it entertains." Educate indeed. What girls learn about is the era-specific products AGP has created for them to buy. It is the education of ensemble and motif. History is recast as the now timeless story of commodity consumption. And commodity consumption is egalitarian. It is as fully realized in the world of Addie, the slave girl doll who escapes to Philadelphia during the Civil War, and Josefina, the somewhat ambiguously labeled "Hispanic" doll, as it is of Samantha, the upper-crust New York doll.

When the shoppers weary of their experience, they can recover at a restaurant that provides special doll seats and tea service, as well as an upscale *pris fixe* menu. Watching people go through American Girl Place—overwhelmingly the shoppers are mother and daughter—is a fascinating experience. Whether dressed in American Girl garb or not, everyone is well turned out. Coming to AGP is obviously a big event for them. There is a distinct aura that envelops those who enter this place, one for which they seem primed. From the moment shoppers are welcomed by the concierge, the sense that those entering are part of an exclusive club is palpable. How privileged one feels to be an American Girl! Once there, however, panic and angst often set in. There is so much to buy, so little time. Truly, these are American girls. They are well prepared for the years of shopping that lie ahead.

The induction of children into the consumer culture is now officially sanctioned by the nation's institutions of public education. Channel One, a profit-seeking commercial newscast designed for children, is shown in more than 40 percent of today's public classrooms. Corporations generate learning materials that also introduce children to company products. In 1999, McGraw-Hill, one of the nation's largest textbook companies, introduced a math text that included product advertisements. Ads adorn school buses and book covers. Corporations sponsor a variety of school contests designed to display and market their products.

Recently a Colorado Springs school district signed a 10-year, $8 million contract with Coca Cola, promising to consume 1.68 million bottles of Coke products in exchange for the money. When the district children did not consume at the needed rate, a superintendent, calling himself the "Coke Dude," sent a memo to school principals urging them to locate Coke machines more conveniently and to allow Coke consumption in class. In Georgia recently, a school accepted a grant from Coca Cola. In exchange for this, the children dressed in Coke T-shirts and formed the company logo for an advertising photo. Just prior to the photographer's snap, one child pulled off his Coke shirt, revealing a shirt with a Pepsi logo. He was disciplined and sent home by school authorities. In modern Georgia, a rebel is one who advertises Pepsi instead of Coke.[6]

By the time they reach college, students are obviously well-versed in the conventions of the consumer mentality. In college, the effort to keep them on track is growing in intensity. In the late eighties, college students became a major target of credit card companies. Today campuses are saturated with credit card promotions, offering a variety of freebies to students who sign up. When these efforts were criticized by university administrators because many students were falling deeply into debt, a Mastercard representative responded that it was "critical for young adults to be able to build a credit history."[7]

They are doing so, with a vengeance. A recent survey by Nellie Mae, the nation's largest maker of student loans, revealed that 65 percent of today's undergraduates have credit cards, and 20 percent have more than four cards. In 1998, the average credit card balance for undergraduates was $2,226. This is on top of an average of $12,000 in college loans that come due upon graduation. Today, Americans aged 22 to 33 account for 18 percent of credit card holders, but 25 percent of credit card debt.[8]

Colleges and universities increasingly pay homage to the conventions of consumption. With little thought of what this implies about both education and students, many university administrators encourage the perspective that students are "customers." The difference between "students" and "customers" may seem small, but it is important. Customers need to be pleased, to be enticed, to be flattered. The concept of a university as a social backwater, a place where conventions are challenged and perhaps shattered, a place to struggle with difficult problems and complex, sometimes uncomfortable ideas, is in retreat. On the rise is a university culture ever more devoted to consumption and entertainment—a kind of "Club Ed."

Mark Edmundson, a professor at the University of Virginia, summarized some of the manifestations of these trends in a recent essay.[9] From the time they are high-school sophomores, students are solicited by college admissions offices that have been remade into marketing machines. Multicolored catalogues and brochures are "customer-friendly" and sprinkled with photographs of students engaged in all sorts of interesting activities. Huge sums are invested in the physical plant of the university to make it aesthetically pleasing, comfortable, and accommodating. Course requirements are reduced, grades inflated, course withdrawal times extended, pass–fail options broadened. Students evaluate the products, and these evaluations are taken quite seriously. Professors are pressured by the laws of the market to make their courses attractive to students, which often means making sure that they are entertaining and not overly demanding. Instead of offering an opportunity to reflect upon such things as the forces that have brought about this social reality, universities are increasingly accommodating to it.

SPORT AND THE BODY POLITIC

At the beginning of the 1999 major league baseball season, owners and the players' association announced that they were discussing whether to allow advertising on baseball uniforms. A senior level baseball executive stated, "We're being meticulous so that we make an intelligent decision. . . . We want to be sure that we do what's in the best interest of baseball." Chicago Cubs pitcher Terry Mulholland humorously claimed that he was holding out for corporate tatoos which, he noted, would require a lifetime contract.[10]

These deliberations were too much for conservative pundit and devoted Cubs fan George Will, who chastised major league baseball for going too far. The problem with Will's analysis is that he skims only the bare surface of the new reality in the world of sport. Throughout history, sports have served a number of important social functions, many of which Will has celebrated in his lifelong devotion to the Cubs. They have provided diversion from the drudgery of work. They promote various human excellences, including grace, beauty, strength, and hard work. They have provided safe outlets for potential hostilities, as in the track and field competition between the United States and the Soviet Union during the peak of the cold war. Sports have provided moral instruction, teaching the virtues of fair play, self-discipline, courage, and honor. Increasingly, however, sports in America is dominated by a newer basic function: Drawing people more deeply into the world of commodity consumption.

As the Baby Ruth candy bar attests, the intermingling of sport and commodity consumption is not new. What is new is the fusion of the two. As previously noted, game rules have been altered to provide more time for advertisements. These have become so integral that TV timeouts are built into some games that are not even being carried on electronic media. On football telecasts, products are now plugged between plays, while the offensive team is huddling. One Monday Night telecast exemplifies the extent of sports commercialization. Although the actual running time for the game was one hour and fifty-two minutes, the telecast lasted three hours and fifteen minutes. During this time commercial breaks came on average every four minutes and nineteen seconds, not including product plugs while the game was running. The network ran 155 ads and network promotions during this telecast.[11]

The starting times of college sports events are altered to conform to the interests of commercial networks. Of course colleges get their cut for doing this. If team fans are inconvenienced, that is a price that will be paid. Increasingly, fans are simply props for the larger huckstering effort anyway. As they vie for a few seconds of TV glory, many eagerly embrace their designated roles, generating signs that contain network logos and that flatter broadcasters. Nor do fans attending games need to worry about spending a couple of hours in an ad-free environment, a condition that might provoke a severe case of the shakes. Today, in sports arenas and ball parks around the country, fans attending games are bombarded with product promotions during any pause in the action.

Commercial interests now attach themselves to sports not only by running ads, but also through broad sponsorships. A corporation will "proudly bring you" Olympic diving, or the American rowing team. College football bowls are now sponsored in such a manner, as are various other sports events. For the first mythic "national championship" football game between Tennessee and Florida State, played at the Tostitos Fiesta Bowl, a Tostitos executive tried to stick a bag of chips into the hand of the winning Tennessee coach during his post-game interview. Let the record show that, to his credit, the coach refused the offer. The NCAA will doubtless soon subject such impudence to sanction. The San Diego Padres broke new ground in 2000 by selling their season to the Sycuan Casino. For that year the Casino "presented" the Padres. Media conglomerates now create sports such as the Winter X Games simply to move goods.

In what may be called the Michael Jordan/Mia Hamm Syndrome, sports heroes are increasingly identified as commodity hucksters. For huge sums of money that now rival or exceed the money they make for playing, athletes endorse products, or don a corporate hat for a post-game interview, or announce their delight in getting to go to Disneyworld. The main function of a sport like gymnastics now seems to be to identify some lucky pixie who will become the next Wheaties poster child. As the worlds of consumption and sport become fused, athletes increasingly accept the idea that they are simply market commodities. The special niche that sports once held in our consciousness gives way to the marketplace. Whether it means jumping from team to team, or leaving school as soon as they are draftable, athletes follow the money. They now sell autographs, which is appropriate because many fans collect autographs simply to sell them.

Sport calls attention to the possibilities of human physical achievement, and, as a byproduct, to the perfection of the human body. And materialism is integrally connected to physical objects as vehicles that refract symbolic meaning. It is not surprising, therefore, that the processes seen in sport, and in the other areas described in this chapter, are also attached to an evolving perspective of the human body. Concerns for appearance are as old as humanity. And it is certainly important to pay attention to one's physical condition. Modern reality goes well beyond this, however, to simulate a true-to-life invasion of the body snatchers. Not only has the body been objectified, today it confronts one as an enemy, a Pandora's box of offending possibilities. It grows too much hair in the wrong places and not enough in the right places, and the hair is too curly, or too straight, or too fine, or too thick. Unsightly bumps appear on its surface. There is too much of it. It smells. Most of all, it ages.

Fortunately, a world of commodities has developed that can help correct the various physical failings that have been made obvious. There is the lure of the "makeover," as advertised on Oprah and other talk shows. Some seek out promising fad diets, diet pills, and diuretics, to more closely approximate the models peering out from the covers of fashion magazines at check-out counters. Others get into body sculpture, pursuing killer abs, or buns of steel. Many are tempted by the more immediate rewards of lyposuction. Or, the body can be made more pleasing by literally altering it physically, through face lifts, nose jobs, breast implants, penis enlargement, fanny tucks, hair transplants, and the like.

Today, specially designed sprays, creams, and gels exist to quell the alleged gaminess of every body crevice and orifice. Spend an hour in the cosmetics and grooming sections of any decent-sized drug store. Notice the iteration of products, the special cream for this patch of skin, the rinse for that type of hair, the deodorant for some particular time of day. It is not surprising, amid this clutter, that the very existence of bodily flesh comes to symbolize a barrier to perfection and satisfaction. As Ewen says ". . . we begin to see that anorexia and bulimia, which are marginalized and diagnosed as eating disorders, are not anomalous, but logical extensions of the norm."[12]

THE ADVERTISED LIFE

The examples of materialist imperialism that have been considered in this chapter could be easily extended. Indeed, the more difficult problem is finding a social sphere that has resisted the intrusion of these values. These examples are part of a much broader process leading to what one observer calls "the advertised life."[13] This is "an emerging mode of being in which advertising not only occupies every negotiable public terrain, but in which it penetrates the cognitive process, invading consciousness to such a point that one expects and looks for advertising, learns to lead one's life as an ad, to think like an advertiser, and even to anticipate and insert oneself in successful strategies of marketing."

The penetration of this ethic to the core of social life leads to an interesting reversal. Traditionally, one's identity has led to the purchase of particular products. Thus, a runner buys running shoes. With increasing frequency, however, it is identity that is purchased in the marketplace. Today a person may buy running shoes in order to be thought of as the kind of person who just might be a runner. The market is no longer simply a place where marketers pay for the right to access potential customers. Customers now eagerly pay for the "right" to wear product logos, to "be like Mike" through our consumption choices, if not in our athletic abilities. One observer has noted the growth of "persona ads."[14] In such ads the point is not to trumpet the quality of the product, but to tell buyers the sort of person they will become by acquiring it. Some persona ads beckon, holding out a desired image. Others bludgeon, telling potential buyers how inadequate they are without the product.

There is an ironic element of "dematerialization" in this process, as products are desired not for their material properties but instead for the images they project. Economist Schor notes the role visibility plays in product selection. Her study indicates that we are much more likely to buy expensive products if they are publicly visible than we are if they are not. Underwear from Sears is fine, but shirts from Sears are far less acceptable. Women are more likely to buy expensive lipsticks, which they often display in public, than they are to buy expensive facial cleansers. In fact, the emergence of style has created a perverse relation between price and demand.[15]

In traditional capitalist theory, price moderates demand. As prices rise, demand drops off, eventually to a point of equilibrium. In today's style-conscious world of consumption, however, rising prices on visible items often *stimulate* demand. Thus, even though Evian water is no different, functionally, from tap water, people buy it *because* it is expensive and visible. Its logo conveys status. People seeking to get this charge on the cheap will refill Evian bottles with tap water. In contrast, to express modesty by pouring Evian water into some nondescript container would be pointless.

The seamless quality of the advertised life is readily seen by anyone willing to spend an hour or two at Niketown in an observant mood. Although it is hard to remember, there was a time when Nike was recognized simply as a seller of shoes. Today it is much more than that. Now a trip to Niketown is a quasi-religious experience for many, a sacred pilgrimage. The facade of the Niketown building in Chicago adumbrates a religious cathedral, its very structure suggesting a church. Upon entering, visitors immediately sense that they are on hallowed ground. Scripture, in the form of well-chosen Nike mantras, adorn the walls. A single "Air Jordan" shoe, encased in a well-lighted, rotating glass cylinder, virtually summons awestruck reverence. High overhead is a larger-than-life photo of His Airness ascending heavenward. He is accompanied by lesser apostles, who, of course, are not quite as ascendent. Sales personnel, like clerics, are cloaked in the uniform garb of the Nike order. Even the money changers in this temple are subdued. There are no gaudy displays, no hawking merchants. Shoes may be purchased, and they are purchased in great quantity, but their importance seems unattached to any intrinsic qualities. Like religious icons, they are important for what they symbolize. Clearly the faithful coming to this temple are in awe. Their reverence is revealed in their faces. They leave to spread the message. "I have been to Niketown. I have seen the light."

SOCIAL AND POLITICAL RELEVANCE

The extension of materialist values to unprecedented levels inevitably raises two kinds of "So what?" questions. Both suggest that the argument of this chapter is much ado about nothing. Implicit in one is the conviction that increasing commodification is a good thing. The church establishment in Mexico, for example, argued that corporate sponsorship of the Papal visit was a good deal because otherwise the tab would have been picked up by the government and the Mexican Church. Under corporate sponsorship, the visit was "free," just like the free stuff one gets when signing up for a credit card. Similarly, corporate-sponsored education materials keep taxes down, which is also good.

This view is shortsighted. Money may be moved around in this process, but citizens do not pay less in this system. On balance, they pay more. Corporations are not eleemosynary institutions. They are motivated by one primordial urge: profit maximization. They hire smart people to think very hard about how to achieve this. If corporate moguls were right in their assessment that Papal identification would provide a good return on their investment, then consumers did not win. They lost. Similarly, a study of sponsored education materials found that about 80 percent of them contained "biased or incomplete information" in a way that "favors the company or its economic agenda."[16] Education freebies, in other words, are not free.

The second "So what?" question flows from the first. It recognizes the penetration of materialism into everyday life, that people now commonly seek identity and community through consumption. Because identity and community are universal human aspirations, however, the important thing is to achieve them. Admittedly, there may be other ways to obtain a sense of self, but the means is less important than the end. What does it matter that, in the United States, we mostly define ourselves by the quality and quantity of our consumption?

The answer to this question becomes apparent when one recognizes the differing motivations in commercial exchange. Although the buyer may be interested in identity, the seller is interested in moving the product. The competition for the buyer's dollar is extraordinary and incessant. Identity and community imply stability and peace, qualities that are inimical to The Sale. Sellers must stimulate dissatisfaction and instability in order to move the product. It is ironic that capitalism, which is usually defended by American conservatives who privilege social stability, is a powerful source of social disruption. Identity is necessarily durable. Seeking it through the highly competitive, fluctuating world of commercial exchange is thus problematic. As the process of accumulation is driven forward, it is powered by the "restless desire for purchase, rather than the pleasures of possession."[17]

In the modern economy, identity and sense of self are the true enemies of commercial exchange, even as they are represented as its goals. The more certain one's sense of self, the less susceptible one is to the blandishments of the modern world of consumption. That is why adolescents, for whom issues of personal identity are on the front burner of psycho/social development, are such rapacious consumers. Consumers chase identity and community up a down escalator. New promises of identity constantly emerge underfoot, but as soon as they are engaged, another step appears which in turn quickly vanishes. The consumption "community" is constantly rotating, requiring consumers to continue purchasing simply to keep pace.

The political consequences of this national devotion to consumption are substantial. Perhaps the most obvious of these is the waste this devotion engenders. Today Americans consume far more than their share of the world's finite resources. For example, with 5 percent of the world's population, the United States is responsible for 25 percent of fossil fuel consumption. As the "underdeveloped" world stands poised on the threshold of industrialization, there is growing alarm in the scientific community about what this will mean for the survivability of the planet. Our consumption pattern hardly places us on the moral high ground for leadership. On the contrary, American corporations race to establish beachheads of consumption in "less developed" areas of the world. Surely lectures to South Americans about the importance of maintaining the tropical rain forest ring hollow to them as they see the damage our consumption does to the environment.

As stated at the beginning of this chapter, consumption will always have its attractions. As our lives come to be defined by consumption, however, when we judge ourselves and others by our consumption, enormous waste is inevitable. As Ewen notes, from a marketing point of view, disposability is the "golden goose," as it conflates the act of "using" with "using up."[18] And so, disposability and waste have become what he calls the spine of the system. The Environmental Protection Agency reports that, in 1960, Americans generated 88 million *tons* of waste in the municipal waste stream. In 1996, we generated 210 million tons into that stream. Recovery programs have had a positive impact, but even taking them into account, waste generation almost doubled during this period. On a per capita basis, Americans generated an average of 2.68 pounds of municipal solid waste a *day* in 1960. By 2000 the per capita amount had risen to 4.33 pounds per day.[19]

Such figures are necessarily abstract. A visit to a municipal dump site, or a conversation with a trash collector about what we daily throw away, would give them more meaning. Recycling has reduced the total volume of annual waste significantly, and much attention has been directed toward that end. But the EPA places recycling only third in its hierarchy of proper waste utilization. In second place is reuse, which involves making further use of items (such as jars) within the home. Most important, according to the EPA, is generating less waste in the first place. It is revealing that the two most important ways to reduce waste have received far less attention than recycling. Both of these, directly or indirectly, involve reduced consumption. Recycling on the other hand, is irrelevant to consumption.

A second way the pervasiveness of consumerist values influences politics is in language usage. Words are the primary symbol system of our species, the process through which meaning is identified. Occasionally one hears politicians derisively referred to as "snake oil salesmen," the reference being to those nineteenth-century entrepreneurs who came into town, made extravagant claims about their products in order to sell them, and then quickly left before the disappointment set in. The analogy is fitting. In the world of commerce, competition for the consumer's dollar necessarily leads to verbal extravagance and hype. As Earl Shorris aptly notes: "The aim of the salesman is to deform the language in a proprietary way."[20] The process through which the smallest box of detergent produced has become the "large" size is well known. Such verbal extravagance is considered "normal," part of the detritus through which Americans daily wade.

Two things are politically relevant about this desecration of language. First, since the commercial realm is now our primary place of public discourse—far more important and pervasive than the political realm—it tends to structure all language usage. In part, politicians sell themselves "as if they were bars of soap" because that is the language style of public discourse. Hence the rickety structures politicians propose are morphed into bridges to the twenty-first century. The second political consequence is that, eventually, commercial hype is recognized for what it is, even as it remains seductive. Language in the public realm becomes something that is not to be taken seriously, and thus nurtures cynicism.

In addition to the generation of waste and the corruption of language, our materialist sensibility has a third effect on political life: It directly impacts the allocation of values that is the essence of politics. One may usefully think of societies as having public and private spheres, even though the boundaries dividing them are murky. The goals of these two spheres may be the same—maximizing human happiness—but their means of achieving this end are different. In the public sphere, goals are sought through political and collective action; in the private sphere, they are left to individual initiative and choice.

All societies have both public and private spheres, although there is disagreement about the relative efficacy of the two spheres in bringing about human happiness, and also about what should and should not be included in each realm. In Canada, for example, the decision to buy bread is considered to be a private act, and so the market establishes the price for bread, with consumers either buying it or not, as price and preference dictate. In Mexico, on the other hand, an ethic establishes a universal right to tortillas. Hence, tortillas are part of the public realm, with the government subsidizing their production costs and regulating the price in order to insure that virtually everyone can afford them. It is possible to claim that either Canada or Mexico is "right" in some abstract sense, but such an argument would make little sense to Canadians or Mexicans if it did not conform to the values of their respective cultures.

In the United States, one of the most significant political consequences of the promotion and magnification of materialist values through the consumer society is that it privileges the private sphere as an avenue for maximizing human happiness and undercuts the public sphere as a means to this end. In effect, the advertising system serves as a huge propaganda apparatus on behalf of the private pursuit of happiness. The advertised life is beguiling. Any single ad seems insignificant, even silly. It is not so much that the claims of a single ad are taken literally. Because a savvy public does not literally believe Sure deodorant will turn the user into an irresistible babe magnet, the ad insinuates a false sense of innocence and harmlessness. The fact that the viewer is in on the joke is disarming. The effect of the sea of ads is quite different. Taken together, they systematically cultivate the notion that happiness is a function of private acquisition, a matter of having the things that can be purchased in the market. It is the pervasiveness of ads, and the uniform ad ethic, that exerts power, even as individual ads seem harmless and, in the constant din, recede in our consciousness. The advertised life appears simply as life itself. Someone once observed that, although it is impossible to determine who discovered water, it is unlikely to have been a fish.

Americans are uncomfortable thinking of themselves as victims of domestic propaganda. To us, this is the fate that befalls people living in other societies. Americans clearly understood throughout the cold war that people in the Soviet Union were "unfree"—in part because they were victims of a substantial propaganda apparatus organized by the State. In contrast, Americans think of their country as "the land of the free," by which is meant that people in this country make unfettered, rational choices about "doing their own thing." Yet it has been noted that, in order to be effective, propaganda cannot be recognized as such by those upon whom it is perpetrated.[21] One reason the Soviet Union eventually collapsed is that its citizens always recognized State propaganda for what it was.

Modern advertising in the United States has all the essential properties of a propaganda system. It is obvious that goods can provide pleasure, and thus the claims of the propaganda system contain the element of truth necessary to make it effective. Yet it also distorts truth as it channels desire toward covert ends. The purpose of the system is to sell goods, not to provide pleasure. Its perspective monopolizes communication. Most important, perhaps, the system is not recognized for what it is. The result is that today Americans are consumed with the idea that consumption defines meaning—as the popular bumper sticker has it, "I shop, therefore, I am." One's "standard of living" is determined by changes in one's disposable income. The messages of the propaganda system to which we are incessantly exposed overwhelm us with the doctrine that happiness is exclusively a private pursuit.

In its definition of happiness, the propaganda system undermines pleasures generated by the public sphere. As the significance of disposable income grows under the constant drumbeat that happiness is a function of privately pursued acquisition, people are concomitantly encouraged to see government as the enemy of happiness. Through taxes, it "takes away" our money and so reduces our chances of obtaining happiness. The pleasures of such things as clean streets, extensive and reliable rapid transit, safe public parks, high quality and low-cost day care, clean air, the pleasures of living in a society where all are doing OK, these have their advocates, but they are drowned in the cacophony of private huckstering.

This leads to a fourth political consequence of the preeminence of materialist values—the nature of the national communications structure. Today our mass media system is essentially organized around selling products, and this has a dramatic impact both on what is considered to be "news" and how news is framed. This has always been true for television, whose economic function, selling audiences to commercial advertisers, grew out of the parameters established by radio in the thirties. Newspapers have also had a long tradition of advertising, but as we noted at the outset of this chapter, advertising has emerged to become the major source of revenue for newspapers. One assessment of early twentieth-century newspapers noted that, even during this period, advertising had the effect of "encouraging inoffensive blandness and a general climate of support for the advertiser's world view."[22]

The effects noted at the beginning of this century have grown, as independent sources of revenue through subscriptions have diminished in significance. Even public radio and television have increasingly come under the sway of the corporate dollar. The American system of public broadcasting, underfunded in comparison to Canadian and European counterparts, is also dependent on a political system that is itself structured by private economic power. Those government and public sponsored niches in our communications system that were supposed to provide relief from commercial interests have been unable to do so. With the money strings controlled by a hostile Congress, public stations have had little choice but to turn to commercial sponsorship. Hence ads, and the interests behind those ads, are a growing presence even on public stations.

Any structure inevitably shapes content, and the dependence of our media system on the corporate dollar is no exception. News executives often claim that they "have never been told" not to run a story. This is because they don't have to be told. They are well socialized into the norms of what is and is not news, and these norms establish parameters comfortable to commercial interests.

Fires are good news, and so is crime. Both are dramatic and inoffensive to commercial interests. Crime could be dangerous to these interests if the most obvious fact about it—that it is integrally connected to poverty—was treated systematically by mass media. Careful studies have indicated that the way news is framed affects what viewers feel ought to be done about it.[23] Stories connecting crime to poverty might therefore encourage people to press for a more equitable distributive system. Those benefiting from the current system need not worry, however, for crime is rarely assessed in this manner. Rather, it is typically portrayed as isolated, episodic acts of some individuals or groups.

In the realm of politics, questions of governance, of the authoritative allocation of values, do not dominate the news. Elections and electoral strategies do. If one were to glean a sense of the meaning of politics from national news programming, one would be hard pressed not to conclude that it is a never-ending saga of people seeking office. As politics is filtered through the lens of the mass media, elections appear less as means to assess and resolve social issues than as tactical horse races. Newscasts are filled with assessments of candidate strategies, personality profiles, daily events, up-to-the-minute polls and the like. When they do appear in campaign news coverage, issues are often treated as strategic efforts of candidates seeking to appeal to one group or another. Such stories serve a two-fold purpose: Since they are about events in the political world, they are accepted by the public as "news." Simultaneously, they represent the kind of news that is inoffensive to commercial interests.

Once in office the activities of politicians, policy-making and otherwise, are mostly personalized—assessing whether they strengthen or diminish a politician's hand. The structuring of the story about the defeat of President Clinton's public health care initiatives in 1992 provides a typical example. This story was portrayed as a stunning personal defeat for the President, and there was much analysis of what "went wrong." Most of this analysis focused on the tactics of the Clinton team, and the response of Congress. Rather than assess what this meant in terms of the struggle over the distribution of values—that is, politics—the air waves were filled with assessments about Clinton's tarnished political image. The episode seemed not to have been about politics at all, except in the narrowest strategic and electoral sense.

There was a political dimension to this story. Private insurance corporations and professional medical associations had spent an unprecedented amount of money to defeat this legislation. Members of Congress were showered with campaign contributions. Chunks of time and space were purchased from media corporations in order to instill doubt in the minds of voters about this initiative. Those who stood to gain from it— mainly the 44 million Americans without health insurance—did not have the resources to purchase equal time. The mass media seemed to be covering the story. It occupied a significant amount of news space. But as a vital link in the commercial chain, indeed as an industry that is now dependent on moving goods, the mass media contorted the news story in a way that did not call attention to their own contribution to the outcome they were reporting.

Perhaps the most ominous political effect of the creeping materialism described in this chapter is the transformation of public roles played by ordinary people. The American Consumer is replacing the American Citizen as the major national archetype. It is important to understand what is lost in this transformation. There are those who argue that, in America, the consumer is king. In a sense this is true. Products come and go, television programs live or die, fortunes are gained or lost, based on the whimsy of the American Consumer. And so consumers are flattered and cajoled, and huge sums are spent trying to figure out how to please them. Their paths are strewn with an endless array of products from which to choose. Although the consumer smiles on this or that product, the process is essentially passive. The only question is, which items on the banquet table will be sampled?

The replacement of the Citizen by the Consumer has ironically been abetted by the consumer movement.[24] Sparked by Ralph Nader's investigation of the Chevrolet Corvair in the sixties, this movement has had some salutary social effect. No one would deny that it is better to have products that actually work and that are not deceptively dangerous. The problem is that this is an extremely limited vision of public responsibility. It encourages the view that the problems of Americans are primarily the problems of getting good exchanges in the marketplace. It raises no questions about consumption itself. In a perverse way, it draws people more deeply into a consumer consciousness.

In contrast to the role of the Consumer, that of the democratic Citizen is not passive. It requires engagement, reflection, assertion, and the like. For the engaged and knowledgeable citizen, the arena of democratic politics at least holds out the possibility for more genuine choice, the occasion to more profoundly exercise freedom. And yet today, as the values of consumerism have come to dominate the political realm, Consumer-Citizens show few of the qualities Jefferson had in mind. They are passive and flattered. Politicians vie mightily for their attention, but little is expected of them beyond choosing from among the images that pass in front of them. This could be the ultimate triumph of materialist values. When the choice among politicians is not based upon policy deliberations, but is simply like a choice between Cheer and Tide, democratic politics is emptied of meaning and democracy itself flounders.

NOTES

1. Data are from December 15, 1998, NBC 7:30–8:30 PM and Fox 10:00–11:00 PM; and January 12, 1999, ABC 9:30–10:30 AM and CBS 10:35–11:35 PM. Viewing was done in Chicago, IL.
2. Ben Bagdikian, *The Media Monopoly*, Boston, MA: Beacon Press, 1997.
3. This account of the Papal visit was taken from "Papal Visit Draws Criticism," John Ward Anderson, *The Washington Post*, January 22, 1999, p. A27.

4. Stuart Ewen, *All Consuming Images*, New York: Basic Books, 1988, p. 241.
5. Victoria J. Rideout, Ulla G. Foehr, Donald F. Roberts, Mollyann Brodie, "Kids & Media@thenewmillennium," a Kaiser Family Foundation Report, November, 1999.
6. Examples of increasing commercialization in schools are taken from "Profits R Us," *Phi Delta Kappan*, George R. Kaplan, November, 1996, pp. K1–K12; "Classrooms For Sale," Nadya Labi, *Time*, April 19, 1999, pp. 44–45; Steven Manning, "Students For Sale," *Nation*, September 27, 1999, pp. 11–18.
7. Mary Geraghty, "Students, Wooed by Credit-Card Purveyors, Often Over-Commit Themselves, Colleges Find," *The Chronicle of Higher Education*, November 8, 1996, pp. A37–38.
8. James Welsh, "Students' Plastic Leads to Life of Debt," *Times-Picayune*, June 22, 1997, F1.
9. Mark Edmundson, "On the Uses of a Liberal Education," *Harper's Magazine*, September, 1997, pp. 39–49.
10. Chip Scoggins, "Is Nothing Sacred?" *Chicago Tribune*, April 2, 1999, Section 4, p. 1
11. Data are from the ABC Monday Night Football telecast, December 28, 1998.
12. Ewen, *op. cit.*, p. 183.
13. Tom Vanderbilt, "The Advertised Life," *Commodify Your Dissent*, New York: W.W. Norton, 1997, p. 128.
14. Edmundson, *op. cit.*, p. 41.
15. See Juliet Schor, *The Overspent American*, New York: Basic Books, 1998, Ch. 3; and Jackson Lears, *Fables of Abundance*, New York: Basic Books, 1994, Ch. 1, for a discussion of dematerialization.
16. The report "Captive Kids: A Report on Commercial Pressures on Kids at School," published by *Consumer Reports* in 1995, was cited in Steve Manning, *op. cit.*, p. 17.
17. Lears, *op. cit.*, p. 20.
18. Ewen, *op. cit.*, Ch. 10.
19. *Characterization of Municipal Solid Waste in the United States: 1997 Update*, Report No. EPA530-R-98-007, May 1998. See also "Talking Trash," William Rathje, *The Washington Post National Weekly Edition*, February 15, 1999, pp. 22–23.
20. Earl Shorris, *A Nation of Salesmen*, New York: Avon, 1994, p. 223.
21. Jacques Ellul, *Propaganda*, New York: Alfred A. Knopf, 1965.
22. Lears, *op. cit.*, p. 203.
23. Shanto Iyengar, *Is Anyone Responsible?*, Chicago, IL: University of Chicago Press, 1994.
24. See Robert D. Holsworth, *Public Interest Liberalism and the Crisis of Affluence*, Cambridge: Schenkman Pub. Co., 1980, for an excellent summary of this process.

8

Culture and Politics Again

The relationships of the cultural characteristics that have been the subject of this book to U.S. politics may be seen through a mental exercise. Imagine a citizen whose political values have been derived exclusively from the cultural characteristics of individualism, competition, mobility, and materialism. Obviously no such person actually exists because human beings are not simply products of their cultures, and American culture is comprised of more than the four characteristics described in these pages. Nevertheless, it is possible to imagine the prototypical citizen whom these characteristics would generate. That person would be self-absorbed, anxious about his place in the world, and have little sense of connection to others in the society. Each of the characteristics that has been considered encourages such orientations. In turn, self-absorption and social disconnection would tend to steer our prototype away from politics. Since the political world would inevitably be involved with many matters outside his immediate self-interest, at least in the narrow sense in which that interest is likely to be construed, he would most probably find politics "boring."

When the thoughts of our prototype did turn to politics, he would tend to think exclusively in terms of an arena in which narrow self-interest is maximized. A primary motivation would be to outdo others in the accumulation and display of personal material goods. If an act of government were to convey specific benefits to him, he would favor it. Other acts of government that brought only benefits to others, or to future generations, would be looked upon with suspicion. He is likely to think government largely benefits others and merely intrudes on his personal, privatized pursuit of happiness. Thus government would be regarded as an entity that takes his hard-earned money and squanders it on wasteful projects. Living in a world of competitive "others," he would not evince much empathy for them. The "other" would be either irrelevant to one's happiness or a potential opponent to be outdone. Both this social distance and our prototype's personal insecurity would make him quick to see fault in others. Our prototype would not think much about common fates, mutuality, or interdependence, and so it is unlikely he would consider the possibility that government could be a positive force in the extension of freedom and happiness.

Any consideration of political culture is necessarily a distortion, and so a prototype constructed even from prominent cultural characteristics is a distortion as well. In the real world, cultural patterns binding members of groups are complex, multiple, and unevenly spread. Calling attention to a few of these means that others are ignored, and some Americans who read this book may not find much of themselves in it. Nevertheless, even though the prototype discussed above is an abstract construct, if the cultural patterns considered here are in fact socially powerful, if they do comprise the building blocks of a dominant culture, such orientations ought at least to be familiar. The prototype should be recognizable.

While the characteristics of individualism, mobility, competition, and materialism do not summarize an exhaustive treatment of U.S. culture, the argument of this book is that they do represent powerful and distinctive ideas growing out of a shared historical experience. Cultural myths are human constructs that are used to explain reality. To some extent, therefore, they must be in sync with that reality, and this book has tried to show that there are good reasons why these patterns developed. Furthermore, these values continue to be cultivated and nurtured in present-day institutional and social experience. Americans grow into them, and use them to make sense of the world. In one degree or another, each of these values may be seen in many of the world's cultures, but their most dramatic expression is manifest in the United States. Hence the values that have been described are *distinctively* American. This nation is easily the most individualistic, the most mobile, the most competitive, and the most materialistic nation in the world.

Each of the political curiosities discussed in Chapter Two—the widespread indifference to politics, the lack of generosity in foreign aid and domestic welfare (combined with the sense that these commitments are in fact substantial), the high levels of crime coupled with a punitive penal system, the uniquely unequal system of wealth and income distribution— is illuminated by the cultural context through which Americans make sense of the world. These curiosities become more familiar, less "curious," when they are placed against the American cultural landscape.

THE CAR AND AMERICANA

For the purposes of analysis, I have treated the dominant characteristics of the culture separately, but they are often fused in the experience of everyday life. Most of the time people experience the whole cloth of a culture, rather than its individual threads. The car is a nice expression of this fusion. If one were looking for an apt metaphor for American culture, some artifact that seemed to embody its core characteristics, one could easily select the automobile. Some of the cultural values discussed in this book are inherent in the car; others are ascribed to it.

The primary purpose of the car is movement, and Chapter Five discusses how enthusiasm for it is in part linked to the value Americans place on *mobility*. In theory at least, the car maximizes geographic mobility in a modern industrial society. It makes accessible regions that could not be easily approached through other forms of transit. When General Motors aired the slogan "See the USA in your Chevrolet" in the earliest days of television, they were following a well-established industry tradition of connecting the acquisition of an automobile to this value. This theme still resonates powerfully in present-day marketing strategies. The automobile clearly embodies the sense of a people "on the move." It is also a major symbol of social mobility. The auto hierarchy adumbrates the social hierarchy. Buying a better car often indicates that one is also making social progress in the world.

Social mobility shades into another of the dominant cultural characteristics: *materialism*. The car represents a substantial personal investment, and clearly this acquisition represents more than a means of physical mobility. Writing at the beginning of the automobile age, social critic Thorstein Veblen noted that the display of social status was an early impetus for buying a car.[1] The car has become a physical embodiment of the good life. Consider how it is marketed. Some ads promote values, such as reliability and comfort, that are intrinsic to the car itself. But as competition for the consumer dollar has grown, auto manufacturers have increasingly attached the purchase of a car to important human values not intrinsic to the car. As with so many other goods in a materialist society, cars are purchased in part to feel better about one's self. Automobile purchase is still considered to be primarily a male activity. Hence male-oriented media such as Monday Night Football and *Esquire* magazine prominently feature car ads. The values connected to cars through these ads extend well beyond the intrinsic properties of cars to include freedom, power, control, social status, sexual potency and fulfillment, and escape. A good car, in short, does more than put one on the fast track to the good life. It *is* the good life.

Automobility is connected to *competition* in two important ways, each of which is actively promoted in marketing strategies. First, car purchases are competitive, as buyers seek to keep up with, or inch ahead of, those in their reference groups. Automobile companies have traditionally come out with new, updated and improved models on an annual basis. In recent years this process has become even more frequent, although the Fall unveilings are still major events. The unrelenting recasting of automobiles is ideally suited to hype competition. People commonly announce the year their car was manufactured as a way to identify it—as in '98 Malibu. Such identification also helps to locate the owner in specific and significant social space.

The car reflects the cultural value of competition in a second way because, for many, the act of driving is highly competitive. The vision of driving as a form of competition is also exploited and encouraged in the promotion of the car. The highway is represented as an eternal challenge, best conquered by the perfect fusion of man (and now also woman) and machine. In addition, other motorists often become the immediate enemy, with drivers constantly seeking to gain advantage over their rivals. Normally civil people seem to experience personality changes behind the wheel of a car—pounding dashboards, swearing, administering obscene gestures to rivals, and so forth. Occasionally such competition can become deadly, as road rage has emerged as a serious social problem. It is hard to understand what causes this seeming transformation—perhaps it is a sublimation, a chance to get even when things have not gone well. Perhaps the highway itself lays social relations bare, as autonomous, isolated individuals struggle to get ahead on the road and in life. For whatever reasons, both in their acquisitions and their use, automobiles are used to express competitiveness.

Finally, the car is an excellent expression of *individualism*. The term "automobile" is apt, as it implies autonomous movement. Undoubtedly one reason the automobile has become such a popular form of transit in this country is because individualism is so important to us. The endless iteration of styles and features serve individualist sensibilities, allowing consumers to feel that they have acquired a special car built just for them. As important, the car allows for highly flexible private movement. It caters to private whim, taking drivers precisely where they wish to go. Driving a car also reinforces privacy and separation. Automobility expresses the desire for loose social bonds. The car also contours social reality, creating what some have called the "drive-thru" culture. It thus increases individualist isolation even as it expresses it.

The automobile is also an apt cultural metaphor because it reflects some of the anxieties associated with the cultural characteristics that have been discussed. It was previously noted that the prototypical citizen distilled from the pure amalgamation of these characteristics would likely be riven with anxiety. In a like manner, the happiness cars extend is ephemeral, and soon drowned in a rising tide of anxiousness. The possibility of getting a "lemon" is a source of continuing angst. Recognizing that cars are not designed to last, people worry that their car will soon fall apart. They fear being swindled by unscrupulous hucksters, and that car warranties are, in practice, worthless. Indeed, the car dealer has become one epitome of sleaze in contemporary society, rivaling the politician for this dubious honor. Rather than expressing freedom, cars often seem more like prisons, as people spend hours steaming on clogged interstates. Theft becomes a major worry, and, increasingly, people turn to car alarms, "clubs," and the like. The car's first dent often induces melancholy in the owner. Even if all these fears were to prove groundless, the car's status is inevitably reduced as new models roll off the assembly line. Ineluctably, the momentary ticket to ultimate fulfillment evolves into just another used car.

The anomalies associated with the automobile are aptly summarized by juxtaposing reality and one of the most popular *mise-en-scènes* of industry advertising: the wilderness. In such ads, cars are found spiriting the driver along a remote desert road, negotiating rugged off-highway terrain, or sitting improbably atop some natural monument. The reality is that no technology has been more destructive of such areas than the car. Auto advertisers promise what the car has taken away. Like the culture itself, cars do not deliver the goods.

CULTURE STRAIN

There is not much of a positive identity generated by the cultural characteristics that have been discussed. Identity is in fact problematic, existing on a horizon line that remains just out of reach. It is not very clear why people have come together, or what they are supposed to share beyond some common urge to be left alone. For much of this nation's history such orienting characteristics have been sustainable. The very vastness of the nation lent plausibility to an anti-social ethic. Industrialization cut in different ways against this ethic. On one hand, it diminished the plausibility of anti-social norms, as people obviously became much more interdependent. In consequence, the Industrial Revolution did spark socialist and reform movements that sought to reconstruct the social story along the lines of common interests and fraternity. These had some effect, but they were unable to generate a vision that was sufficiently compelling to achieve a position of cultural dominance. The more powerful impulse of the American Industrial Revolution, on the other hand, cut in a different direction. It promoted the idea that the good life was to be achieved through the private consumption of products. Recognizing, at least tacitly, that product movement is enhanced by individualist, competitive, and mobile norms, industrialists sought to extend these features of the culture.

Despite the efforts to sustain the dominant culture, there has been growing pressure in the social relationships of daily life for ameliorative social policies. In the last fifty years government programs providing various kinds of assistance—including Social Security, Medicare, Student Financial Aid, Head Start, the Clean Water Act, Federal Emergency Management, and Americorps—have risen and prospered in the face of normal impulses generated by the dominant culture. Critics might argue that these programs only scratch the surface of what needs to be done, that they are jerry-built, ad hoc structures, and thus that the culture has in fact been substantially constraining. Nevertheless, the existence of such programs does bespeak an underlying, if amorphous, sense of mutuality.

The American welfare state is minimal by standards of other industrial nations. Yet, with the outstanding exception of programs designed to assist the nation's poorest (and politically weakest) citizens, it has withstood serious assault. This fact provides further evidence of some discomfort with the dominant political culture. Despite their ascendancy, conservative politicians in the last decades of the twentieth century were unable to reduce significantly the size of the welfare state. Political conservatives are the most ardent advocates of the dominant norms of the culture, and conservative rhetoric has faithfully advocated these values. "The government cannot solve problems," President Reagan once proclaimed, "the government *is* the problem." Conservatives regularly inveigh against the welfare state, proposing in its place the creation of an "Opportunity Society." "Personal Responsibility" is another frequent theme animating their policy proposals. Such phrases resonate nicely with the dominant culture, and extensive polling convinced conservative leaders in Congress that they were highly popular with the public as well.

Despite the popularity of such familiar cultural themes, the public balked at actions seeking to convert them to policy. When conservative Republicans gained control of Congress in the elections of 1994, the time appeared right for a serious assault on the welfare state. Several of the items in the "Contract with America"—a series of policy proposals Republicans promised to implement if they gained a majority in the 1994 Congressional elections—were attacks on interventionist government policy. With polls showing President Clinton's approval ratings dipping below 40 percent, the Republican leadership in the House of Representatives began to push hard for the implementation of the Contract. As they did, however, President Clinton's popularity began almost immediately to rebound.

When Republicans proposed to bring the budget in balance by making deeper cuts in social spending than the President wanted, the conflict edged into a crisis that briefly closed "nonessential" operations of the government. At this point public support turned decisively in the direction of President Clinton. Thus policies that resonated with the dominant culture and that seemed popular at a general rhetorical level proved unpopular when they were specified.

The work of sociologist Alan Wolfe reveals that middle-class Americans are in fact troubled by unfettered capitalism. Through a combination of standardized questionnaires and in-depth interviews, Professor Wolfe led a research study of modern middle-class suburbanites. He found the expected antipathy toward labor unions. What surprised him was that his respondents evinced substantial hostility toward business.[2] He summarized their most representative sentiment as "balanced capitalism," which has three components. Middle-class Americans now expect corporations to balance their self-interest with the need to consider what benefits the larger society. Second, they want corporate life to be organized so that people can balance their obligations to work with their obligations to family, church, and community. Third, they believe that corporate executives should be compensated in ways that are not out of balance with "common sense and moral proportionality." Wolfe found that the middle class judges corporate America to be out of balance in each of these three areas.

In a similar vein, Richard Sennett[3] calls the behavior of the modern American corporation into account. The modern corporation, Sennett believes, has had an ironic impact. By undercutting place and community, it has created an intense longing for them. Sennett's personal reflections are underscored by Wolfe's interviews with middle-class suburbanites. The interviews, Wolfe reports, are laced with comments about the lack of community in their lives. And the respondents are equally clear about the reasons for the eclipse of community:[4] "If there has been an eclipse of community, the cause is the work place. So great have become the demands of the job that the obligations of the neighborhood have had to give way." Perhaps the best evidence for both the eclipse of, and the yearning for, community is found in the extent to which the modern corporation relies on the values of community and place to sell its products.

Sennett argues that the rationale for the corporation must change. The corporate ledger of profit and loss must be subsumed by the consideration of the value of the corporation to the community and how it serves civic interests. His concluding chapter notes that a place becomes a community when people use the "dangerous" pronoun "we." "To speak in this way requires a particular though not a local attachment; a nation can constitute a community when in it people translate shared beliefs and values into concrete, daily practices."[5]

CULTURAL PERSISTENCE

Technological innovations and continued industrial development in the twentieth century stimulated both greater vulnerability and greater interdependence. In the face of increasingly obvious mutuality, it is interesting to consider why a more compelling cultural story has not been generated in the United States. Cultures are, after all, human constructs through which people make sense of their world. How is it that cultural constructs that do not seem to resonate with actual experience in the everyday world nevertheless powerfully persist? A number of factors contribute to answering this question.

First, although cultures are human constructs, not all participate equally in their construction and propagation. The anti-social character of the dominant political culture works to the advantage of those who are already the most favored in the society. Individualism ratifies the status quo. It bestows legitimacy on those who have "made it" and shows those who are in disadvantaged positions that their problems are private. Competition and mobility work much in the same way and, in addition, distance people from each other. Materialism directs attention toward a conception of the good life as a function of private, profit-driven activities. Each of these characteristics steers people away from a system of mutual guarantees and protections and toward private, competitive striving. It is hardly surprising that those who benefit from these cultural arrangements have little interest in cultural reformulation. A culture that devalues commonality, that instead sets people against each other in a depoliticized world, confers huge advantages upon those in the most privileged positions of the society. As Christian Bay has noted,[6] for all its imperfections, it is the political realm that best offers hope to average and disadvantaged citizens for redressing grievances against the social order.

Second, if the cultural characteristics have not been especially fruitful in generating a sense of interdependence and commonality by conveying to Americans who they *are*, Gitlin[7] has convincingly argued that for much of the twentieth century, unity was largely constructed around who they are *not*. He notes that World War I generated a fierce nationalism bordering on xenophobia. The nation largely united in its opposition to alien forces, which were perceived as threatening Americans at home as well as abroad. During World War II, popular culture joined in the war effort, uniting disparate Americans against the common enemy. Gitlin cites film historian Jeanine Basinger on the clear moral generated by Hollywood war movies during this time:[8] "We are a mongrel nation—ragtail, unprepared, disorganized, quarrelsome among ourselves, and with separate special interests, raised, as we are, to believe in the individual, not the group. At the same time, we bring different skills and abilities together for the common good, and from these separate needs and backgrounds we bring a feisty determination."

The common sense of purpose that was necessary to wage a successful war did have some residual social benefits. A grateful nation extended substantial housing and educational benefits to returning GIs, allowing them to move into the middle class in unprecedented numbers. Here, it would seem, was an opportunity for a national conversation about the possibility of constructing a positive national identity, but this was not to be. Television, arriving on the scene in the post-war years, was a major force in propping up the dominant characteristics of the culture, particularly its consumer, competitive, and upwardly mobile aspects.

Just as important, the emerging forty-year Cold War once again brought to center stage the sufficiency of negative identification. Americans knew that they were not Commies, and anti-communism became the bedrock of unity. Potential challenges to the dominant culture, and to social and economic inequities generated under its purview, were stifled. Charges of collectivism, socialism, communism, were leveled against individuals, programs, and ideas that suggested mutual obligations. Labels such as "soft on communism" and "pinko"—hardly nuanced contrasts to the virile manliness the dominant culture supposedly expressed so well—filled the air. "UnAmerican" activities and individuals—a truly ironic concept in a nation supposedly revering freedom—were monitored and subverted by various agencies of the government and by nongovernmental guardians of the culture as well.

Still, there were rumblings from below. African Americans, briefly pulled into the American mainstream by the urgency of the Second World War, found, after the completion of the war, that they were expected to return to their traditional second-class status in the society. They soon renewed their long struggle for social justice with great intensity. The controversial war in Vietnam stimulated substantial anger and opposition. Many in the civil rights and antiwar movements began to locate the reasons for racial injustice and for the war in the dominant culture, and the sixties saw the emergence of what was called the "counterculture." Some elements of both black and antiwar movements were secessionist, encouraging young black and white counterculturalists to drop out of mainstream society and to form principled and sustainable alternative living groups. Other parts of the counterculture were openly confrontational with the dominant culture.

Always a potpourri of conflicting attitudes and styles, much of this movement was less radical than most of its critics and members believed. At its best, it was a noble effort. Generous in spirit, it raised serious questions about the direction of society. It challenged the cultural norms of materialism, competition, and social mobility. Many members of this movement reconstructed their lives around alternative binding norms, and many continue to live by those norms today. At its worst, the counterculture was arrogant, intolerant, and self-indulgent, an adolescent fantasy of fun without responsibility. Such attitudes had much in common with the dominant culture against which there was a supposed rebellion. The national media, more interested in entertainment than in discourse, tended to give attention to the more frivolous parts of this "movement," and another opportunity for dialogue about binding norms was eclipsed.

Finally, a conversation about a reconstituted culture that recognizes interdependence and mutuality has been impeded by what Gitlin and others have called the "balkanization of the left." Just as the guardians of the dominant culture have tended to be conservatives, cultural criticism has traditionally been the province of the left. (Here we are not thinking of "popular culture," which many conservatives criticize.) In the United States, issues of inclusion, mutuality, equality, and interdependence have traditionally been raised by political progressives. Their vision of humanity has pointed to an essentially common human condition. In contemporary U.S. political life, however, it is "multiculturalism" and social group dignity, not common vision, that has become the central concern of progressives.

There is much to be said for the rise of multiculturalism in the United States. It is an invaluable response to ignorance. It enhances the dignity of many who have been ignored by society even as it reduces that ignorance. But multiculturalism becomes problematic when it evolves into identity politics, which deduces positions or a way of life from a fact of birth, sex, national origin, physical disability, or the like. As generators of difference, the group is a category that cannot be transcended. It is a product of what Gitlin calls "binary thinking," in which people are declared to be part of Group X, not Group Y. Ironically, while it forestalls general commonality, it inflates group commonality, requiring members of a particular group to march in lock step while proclaiming how different they are. Why it is that these groups generate identity, while other more particular or more general groups do not, is obscure.[9]

In the meantime, artists like Amy Tan, Spike Lee, Sandra Cisneros, and Toni Morrison are compelling because they work against stereotypes, shedding light on the varieties of human experience within differing social groups. The work of such artists pays homage to group dignity, but also reveals universal commonalities and truths. Identity politics, on the other hand, tends to freeze people in groups. Sometimes these groups may form tactical alliances; sometimes they are in opposition. But it is the discrete group that defines essential reality. A progressive movement without universalist claims is, quite simply, not a progressive movement.

CULTURAL EVOLUTION

Thus the dominant culture limps along. Beset by a world for which its explanations are less and less compelling, it is nevertheless pushed relentlessly by those seeking to sustain the current social order. The existence of an "other" for most of the twentieth century has papered over cultural strains by providing unity through opposition. Progressives, who might be expected to articulate cultural ideals of commonality, have instead produced a cacophony of specific group claims. Still, it is important to recall that cultures are creative constructs, reflective reactions to the world that people find around them. They also exist in a dynamic relationship with the imagination. Cultures are produced by imaginative thought, even as they serve to limit it. People think, but their ideas do not spring from virgin soil. To paraphrase Gitlin paraphrasing Marshall Berman paraphrasing Trotsky, although you may not be interested in culture, culture is interested in you.[10]

At the same time, people's cultural experience does not determine definitively who they are. It is not simply Kenneth Burke's definition of human beings that makes this so. The truth of the simultaneous human passions for both order and novelty is revealed in history. Given the inadequacy of the dominant culture in explaining present reality, the ground now occupied by it will be increasingly contested and perhaps eventually reconstituted and reformulated. It is unlikely this would be accomplished through a collective national epiphany that induces a sharp, fundamental change in culture. Not that the efforts of those trying to induce such an epiphany are necessarily misplaced. The most significant difference between culture and ideology is that, while ideologies are consciously formed and espoused, cultures are not. They provide the "deep structure" for interpreting the world, and are experienced as reality itself. The act of calling cultural values to account also brings them to the surface of consciousness. To reveal culture as "mere" ideology may be an important step in its reformulation. Still, instances of "cultural revolution" in human history have been comparatively few, and most of these have been pretty unpleasant. It is far more likely that older cultural norms will wither away, dying the death of a thousand cuts.

Toward the end of his study of the American middle class, Professor Wolfe muses over an interesting conundrum: When discussing social welfare, his respondents framed their discontent around the norm of personal responsibility. Yet when discussing the faults of government, or big business, the respondents invoked an attitude of "injured self-pity" that allowed them to avoid taking responsibility for their own condition. Wolfe thought it "odd that people who believe so much in personal accountability seem to take so little responsibility for what they see as wrong with their society."[11] Cultural battles are always unevenly waged, but in this society powerlessness is a choice.

INDIVIDUAL CHOICE AND CULTURAL CHANGE

On January 30, 1927, the excited members of the Salina, Kansas First Christian Church dedicated their new edifice.[12] For a small town, the building was an extraordinary structure: Gothic brick and limestone, with large arched windows, and an interior featuring walnut beams, oak pews, and fifty stained-glass windows. Over the years, however, the congregation dwindled and the building deteriorated. Rather than shoulder heavy renovation costs, the congregation decided to sell the building and move to a new and smaller location down the road.

Chad Kassem, the owner of Acoustic Sounds, purchased the old church building in 1996. Mr. Kassem needed storage space for his mail-order music catalogue business that specialized in old-time country and blues. He repaired the leaky roof and crumbling walls, and thought of moving in along with his overflow inventory. Soon the building's extraordinary acoustics became apparent, and Kassem was seized with the idea of turning it into a recording studio. In 1998, Blue Heaven Studios was founded, and its unusual physical qualities made it one of the finest recording studios in the nation.

What inspired Mr. Kassem was not the possibility of maximizing his income by this fortuitous string of events. Rather, it was a newborn ability to record old and neglected blues artists in the Kansas area and from the South. "There's no great way to say it," he told the *Salina Journal,* "I want to record them before it's too late." Kassem has been unceasing in his efforts to establish a permanent public record of Little Hatch, Jimmie Lee Robinson, Honeyboy Edwards, Weepin' Willie Robinson, and others who are, in his view, neglected "greats."

The interesting thing about this story from the perspective of this book is how little the cultural characteristics considered here seemed to have influenced Kassem. Certainly one can see an element of individualism. No one, and certainly not the marketplace, is going to define a deserving artist for him. Beyond this, the motivating sentiment is Kassem's strong desire that neglected people in the blues tradition be remembered. He wants others to be connected with this tradition, to understand its roots, and to give these artists the recognition they deserve. Of course he manages to make a living at what he does, but this is not his fundamental motivation. He is creating a gift, a treasure, that he wants to share with the nation.

Many people today, like Chad Kassem, live by values that contradict one or more of the cultural characteristics considered in this book. They are not, of course, a majority, but they are substantial enough to be politically and socially significant. Some, because of their experiences, have never found these dominant characteristics to be compelling. Others have come to a point of consciously rejecting them as adults. Juliet Schor, whose work chronicling the rise of the "New Materialism" was discussed in Chapter Six, concludes her book with a discussion of people in her sample—almost one-fifth of the total—who have consciously chosen to step off the consumer escalator. This group, whom she labels "voluntary downshifters," made lifestyle changes, excluding regular retirement, that entailed earning less money.[13] They did this because they recognized and valued the things materialism could *not* achieve in their lives. This quite heterogeneous group includes people across economic income brackets. Ideologically it is diverse, too, ranging from philosophically committed simple livers, to environmental activists, to people who simply want to have more time for family and community.

Others, despite growing time pressures, continue to give their time and talents in voluntary service activities of extraordinary variety. Because these efforts are so local and disparate, they are often hidden from view. They are rarely regarded as newsworthy. Today's college students are probably more politically disconnected than any previous generation, and they are often characterized in the mass media as anti-social airheads. Yet volunteerism on college campuses is thriving. In a recent poll, 71 percent of college students reported engaging in such volunteer activities as helping the homeless, teaching, religious service, social work, the environment, and health care. Forty-one percent said they had volunteered more than 10 times.[14] Clearly, many students today are looking for ways to connect themselves to the larger society—if not to its politics.

At a very different level, some people of substantial means show strong senses of social obligation. Ted Turner gave a huge sum of money to the United Nations, and caused great confusion in the national media over how to treat such an unusual gesture. In Minnesota, Kenneth and Judy Dayton, of the Dayton Department Stores, developed a personal nine-step plan of philanthropic giving. In 1998, they achieved step seven, which was capping their wealth. Any income they receive over their cap now automatically goes to charity. The next step in their plan is to reduce their wealth, and then to leave almost all of their assets to nonprofit organizations. Mr. Dayton is active in an organization that seeks to get other wealthy citizens of Minnesota to increase their charitable giving. In an interview he refused to divulge either his wealth or his level of giving, saying, "I don't think anyone of wealth has any right to gloat over what they give because the poor do such a better job of giving than the wealthy do, as a percent." According to a 1999 Gallup Poll, families earning less than $10,000 a year gave 5.25 percent of their income to charity; families with incomes in excess of $100,000 gave 2.2 percent.[15]

Evidence of growing social consciousness can even be found, of all places, in market investing. A recent report by the Conference Board, a private business research group based in New York, showed a growing concern for "moral investing." Increasingly, investors are looking for companies whose work is considered by them not socially harmful. In response, an estimated 160 mutual funds invest in screened, "socially responsible" companies. Between 1995 and 1997, investments in such portfolios grew at a rate of 229 percent. This compared favorably to the overall pension fund growth of 84 percent.[16]

Such "countercultural" examples could easily be multiplied. Throughout the country, many people make individual choices that seem to contradict the norms of the dominant culture. Sometimes these choices occur because of the adoption of shared norms from subsets of the society—churches, communities, ethnic groups, and the like. Sometimes they are the products of reflective thought. It is tempting to dismiss them because they are so disparate. They are not organized, not part of a movement, and they are not dominant. And yet any decision, no matter how small, to live by values other than those generated by the dominant culture, creates an awareness in others that such a life is possible. It is through such awareness that cultures sometimes evolve.

Even a cultural value as deeply ingrained as materialism is not unassailable. The discussion of the imperialism of materialist values in the last chapter painted a depressing portrait. On one hand, these values have been so promoted through various social institutions, but especially by television, that they now thoroughly saturate society. Truly, most Americans seem to be leading what has been called "the advertised life." On the other hand, materialist values logically require the subversion of human happiness. Happiness must remain evanescent, something people pursue but never obtain. And so there appears to be no escape from this dilemma. The only response seems to be, as the grinning fool in the beer commercial has it, "Why ask why?" Given the advertised life, the levels of consumption in America are hardly surprising. What is remarkable is, after a lifetime of near total immersion in consumerist values, how many people, when confronted with the question, "Aren't these values shallow and empty?" will instantly recognize that they are.

The first step in gaining control of a cultural value such as materialism is to recognize that it *is* a cultural value, a social construct. One way to do this, in families and schools, is to deconstruct ads, thus calling attention to their real purpose. Individual ads might be assessed and deconstructed. For example, people could be encouraged to think about the meaning behind such lunacy as the mass media's rating of Super Bowl ads. What, exactly, *is* a "good" ad? Efforts could also be made to eliminate the public subsidy for advertising by eliminating postal rate breaks for junk mail, as well as the tax write-off for advertising. Such efforts would face significant political opposition, but merely having them on the agenda would call attention to this system and thus create greater space for choice.

Another way to combat the advertised life is through the creation and extension of "ad-free" zones in the public sphere. As public institutions, schools are not a bad place to begin. But ad-free zones are especially important for television, which is now the most important means through which Americans receive a sense of who they are. Some radical critics of television have called for its elimination, arguing that the problem is not *what* we watch on TV, but *that* we watch.[17] This is neither desirable nor possible. But it is certainly desirable and possible to create a television system whose sole purpose is not simply to attach viewers to the market. To this end, technology has become an important ally. The spectrum, which until a few years ago sharply limited the number of channels available in a given area, has exploded. Now hundreds of channels are potentially available in every television market.

Reserving one or two channels in every market that are free from both commercial and political pressures, as is done in Great Britain, could be easily accomplished. At present, even American public television is subject to both of these pressures. Relief could be accomplished by changing how public programming is financed. The current system of financing, which combines individual donations (more likely to come from wealthier segments of the population), Congressional budgetary allocations, and, increasingly, corporate advertising, could be supplanted by a system of independent financing. This could be achieved either by a tax on the sales of TV sets or, in exchange for the licenses allowing commercial networks to operate over the public airwaves, a tax on their huge profits. That is how it is done in Britain. One comparative study has shown that the alternative systems of finance have a significant impact on program content.[18] Because such a change would alter the content of what is shown on television, it would also expand the possibilities of political and social discourse.

CHANGING SOCIAL RULES, CHANGING CULTURE

Cultures do not evolve simply in response to individual choice. Their relationship to politics is dynamic and reciprocal. Because cultures establish shared ways of viewing the world, they affect the contours of social policy. But if social policy were merely a function of underlying cultural values, explanation in political science would be much easier. Many factors contribute to the development of social policies, and as this is the case, emergent policy can also encourage rethinking the meaning of human association. For example, a system of publicly financed elections would make politicians far less dependent on private wealth and change the nature of public conversation in this country. Nothing about the dominant culture suggests the possibility of doing this. In the first place, those who immediately benefit from the current system, already-elected politicians, would be required to change it, and politicians are not noted for going against their self-interests. Second, the current system favors wealthy, entrenched interests, which could be expected to represent such a change as a costly "free ride" to politicians at taxpayer expense. In a culture that neither highly values politicians nor encourages taxes, changing the status quo would not be easy.

On the other hand, both surveys and electoral behavior indicate significant popular disgust with the political system. Most of this is directed at politicians, but there is growing recognition that politicians are corrupted by powerful economic interests. And, for their part, many politicians privately despair that so much time must be devoted to begging private interests for campaign money. This unsavory process demeans politicians most of all. The effort to outlaw "soft money" (in effect, unlimited campaign contributions) does not go nearly far enough to break the dominance of private wealth in the political system, but it is a step in that direction, and this legislation almost passed in the most conservative Congress in recent history.[19]

One of the political curiosities discussed in Chapter Two, economic inequality, also illustrates the interconnection of evolving social rules and evolving culture. The vast and growing inequality in America is supported by underlying cultural norms. Any distributive system is the product of rules generated by that system—that is, a product of politics. Perhaps nothing speaks more loudly about the impact of the cultural characteristics discussed in this book than the levels of economic inequality these characteristics not only tolerate but encourage. The social consequences of this are substantial. The distribution system is inevitably a means of self-evaluation and the vast discrepancies in the American system assault self-respect, which the philosopher John Rawls[20] calls "perhaps the most important primary good" of a democratic society. Without self-respect, Rawls argues, "All desire and activity becomes empty and vain and we sink into apathy and cynicism." To this, one could add that it also generates anger and diminishes commitment to the community.

Commitment to the community is also discouraged at the other end of the economic spectrum as well. Disproportionate wealth encourages social withdrawal. With some notable exceptions, the growing trend is for the wealthy to seclude themselves from the normal cares of the larger society. More and more people live in barricaded, private enclaves. They employ their own security forces. Their children go to private schools. They recreate in closed clubs and vacation in private resorts to which they travel in privately owned jets. Their wealth serves as a means to disconnect them from the concerns of the vast majority in the society.

This disconnection may be sought because it is so difficult to justify rationally the malapportionment of the current rewards system. The conventional justification is that distributions are the results of an incentive system that is essential for economic progress and growth. Changing the social rules to reduce economic inequality would deter growth, which would be bad for everyone. The problem for this line of argumentation is domestic and international economic history. All modern nations experience economic cycles of growth and contraction, and these are not correlated with levels of economic inequality.[21]

Syndicated columnist Geneva Overholser recently devoted two columns to economic inequality in America.[22] The first was a discussion of how much better CEOs have done financially in recent decades in comparison to their employees. She noted, for example, that in 1998 alone, pay increases for CEOs of large companies averaged 36 percent, while the pay increase of blue-collar employees was 2.7 percent. She also noted that these increases were not connected to company performance. Her second column was devoted to reader response to the first column. "Not since I vented about sports utility vehicles" she wrote, "have I heard from so many readers pointing out the error of my ways." The responses were overwhelmingly couched in the linguistic symbols of the dominant culture: individualism, merit, hard work, the majesty and fairness of the market, and so forth.

The fact that a mainstream columnist like Overholser raises these questions indicates, despite contrary cultural pressures, a growing uneasiness with the way social rules distribute the fruits of this society. Consider what might seem to be a difficult case, that of Bill Gates. In 1998 Gates, the world's richest person, was worth $90 billion. What makes this case more difficult than many is that he did not inherit his fortune, nor is it the result of some lucky investment in the stock market. Mr. Gates seems to embody the meritorious individualized ideal of the dominant culture, and yet he may also symbolize that culture's decreasing ability to create a compelling social story. Justifying this kind of reward in a land where tens of millions of people have no net wealth at all is increasingly problematic. Even the arch-fiend of the Austin Powers films, Dr. Evil, initially thought to hold the world at ransom for only a MILLION dollars. (After appropriate socialization, he raised his price to $100 billion.) Give Mr. Gates the benefit of the doubt. Allow that he is a genius. Concede that he works extraordinarily hard. Grant that Microsoft has fundamentally changed the society. Assume this change is exclusively for the social good. The conclusion might readily be that Mr. Gates should be very well compensated for his natural talents, for his hard work, and for the social good that he has stimulated. Assuming all of these things, there is still no way to conclude he merits $90 billion. He simply has been the beneficiary of the American social rules of distribution. Mr. Gates himself seems implicitly to recognize this, as he has publicly stated that he is going to give most of his wealth to charity. The question is whether such decisions should be left to the whim of individuals.

There are a number of ways in which the fruits of the society could be more equitably distributed. The system of taxation could become more progressive, as it is in most other economically advanced countries. This could pave the way for a better "social contract" for most Americans. This might include such things as a system of national health care to replace the fragile and uneven system that functionally ties medical insurance to the whimsy of working for an employer who offers a health plan. A safe, reliable, and inexpensive system of public transportation could be established. More, and more equitable, support for public education would contribute to a better social bargain as well.

A few economists and political theorists are beginning to think about the question of more equitable distribution in venues that spill into the public arena. One equalizing strategy, for example, is to reestablish property rights so that each citizen is entitled to a per capita share of the nation's profits in what economist John Roemer calls a "social dividend."[23] Other economists and political theorists have also articulated this idea. Bruce Ackerman and Anne Alstott, from Yale University, have proposed that, upon reaching adulthood, every citizen be given a stake of $80,000. The purpose of this stake would be to help them get started in life, and could be used in any way recipients desired. It could pay for college, or for getting started in business, or for a car and a down payment on a home, or for lottery tickets. At death, there would be a primary obligation to repay the stake. Wealth in excess of this obligation would continue to be passed on in the traditional ways—to families, friends, and charities. Eventually, therefore, the system would become self-supporting, but to get it started, and as long as necessary, a 2 percent tax on wealth is proposed.

Ackerman and Alstott contend that their idea is both realistic and politically feasible, and most of their book is given to assessing the kinds of economic and social objections that one can readily imagine being generated by those steeped in traditional American culture. The plan is not as far-fetched as it might seem initially. Alaska doles out some of the profits from public oil preserves to its citizens, giving each $1,000 every year. This "permanent fund" has become so popular that both political parties in that state have pledged to protect it. And, without the support of the dominant culture, the United States still spends significantly on its children, by investing in schools, on school lunch programs, and the like. Representatives of the government do seem to be willing to take steps to insure that more children, at least, receive medical coverage. And the government makes significant commitments to the elderly, through Social Security, Medicare, and the like. Perhaps making a similar commitment to young adults would increase their stake in the society.

By traditional cultural standards, ideas like a "stakeholder society" are quite strange, and they are certainly not politically important at this point. The main barriers to considering such distribution issues, however, are not rational but cultural, and the fact that such ideas are beginning to enter the public arena is interesting. If discussions of this sort were to evolve, it would likely have an impact on culture, on the patterns of ideas

Americans use to interpret reality. Something like a stakeholder society would require Americans to rethink their story, for it expresses a broad, and common, social commitment.

We close this book with a consideration of the stakeholder society, not out of a conviction that it is the path that ought to be chosen, but because of two things: First, it reflects a culture under stress. The dominant U.S. culture is one that is increasingly out of sync with a world where lives and fates are inevitably shared. Second, this example also illustrates the fact that the relation between culture and social structure is both dynamic and reciprocal. Altering social structure creates new cultural possibilities. A culture of commonality would encourage the consideration of something like the stakeholder society. On the other hand, a broadly shared stake in the society reinforces and extends a culture of commonality. Whether a newly shared vision that encourages the development of our best selves in the context of a humane society will emerge is a question the new millennium will answer.

NOTES

1. Thorstein Veblen, *The Theory of the Leisure Class*, Amherst, NY: Prometheus Books, 1998.
2. Alan Wolfe, *One Nation After All*, New York: Viking, 1998, p. 237.
3. Richard Sennett, *The Corrosion of Character*, New York: W.W. Norton, 1998, pp. 136–148.
4. Wolfe, *op.cit*, p. 251.
5. Sennett, *op.cit.*, p. 137.
6. Christian Bay, "Politics and Pseudopolitics," *The American Political Science Review*, Vol. 59, March 1965.
7. Todd Gitlin, *The Twilight of Common Dreams*, New York: Metropolitan Books, 1995. See especially Ch. 2.
8. Cited in Gitlin, *op. cit.*, p. 60.
9. For a thoughtful discussion of this subject, see Thomas Spragens, Jr., "Identity Politics and the Liberalism of Difference: Missing the Big Picture," *The Responsive Community*, Vol. 9, Issue 3, 1999, pp. 12–25.
10. Gitlin, *op. cit.*, p. 200.
11. Wolfe, *op.cit.*, pp. 313–314.
12. Information for this story was taken from a National Public Radio report on Blue Heaven Studios by Linda Wertheimer on "All Things Considered," in September, 1999. A transcript of this report is available at Burrelle's Transcripts, c/o NPR, P.O. Box 7, Livingston, New Jersey 07039. Historical information was obtained through the Blue Heaven Studios website: www.acousticsounds.com.
13. See Juliet B. Schor, *The Overspent American*, New York: Basic Books, 1998, Ch. 5, for a discussion of downshifters. A more extensive treatment may be found in David Shi, *The Simple Life*, New York: Oxford University Press, 1985.

14. Adam Clymer, "College Students Not Drawn to Voting or Politics, Poll Shows," *New York Times National,* January 12, 2000, p. A14.

15. Robert Franklin, "Daytons reveal decision to cap their wealth; extra income will go to charity," *Minneapolis Star Tribune*, November 12, 1998, p. A1. Gallup Poll data are from Cindy Richards, "Spreading the Wealth," Chicago Tribune Magazine, June 18, 2000, pp. 10–16.

16. James G. Glassman, "A Matter of Morals," *The Washington Post National Weekly Edition*, February 15, 1999, p. 35.

17. See, for example, Jerry Mander, *Four Arguments for the Elimination of Television*, New York: Morrow, 1978, and Marie Winn, *The Plug-in Drug*, New York: Viking Press, 1985.

18. Philip Green, "American Television and Consumerist Democracy," *Dissent*, Spring, 1998, pp. 49–57.

19. For a more extended treatment of this important issue by the author, see J. Harry Wray, "Money and Politics," in *Handbook of Political Marketing*, Bruce I. Newman, ed., Thousand Oaks, CA: Sage, 1999.

20. John Rawls, *A Theory of Justice*, Cambridge: Harvard University Press, 1971, p. 440.

21. Robert Kuttner, *The Economic Illusion*, Boston, MA: Houghton Mifflin, 1984.

22. Geneva Overholser, "He or she who rules," *The Chicago Tribune*, November 10, 1999, Section I, p. 27.

23. John Roemer, "Egalitarian Strategies," *Dissent*, Summer, 1999, pp. 64–74. Bruce Ackerman and Anne Alstott, *The Stakeholder Society*, New Haven, CT: Yale University Press, 1999.

Index